LEVEL UP

TURNING YOUR OBSTACLES
INTO SUPERPOWERS

Arina,

Very excited to have you on the team! I'm sure
we are going to grow together and build something
great. May this book empower you to LEVEL UP
towards your dream life—

Best,

ALVARO NUÑEZ ALFARO

ISBN: 978-1-951503-97-0 (Paperback)
ISBN: 978-1-951503-98-7 (Ebook)

Author photo credit: Daniele Venturelli

Authorsunite.com

"The biggest adventure you can ever take,
is to live the life of your dreams."
~ Oprah Winfrey ~

For all the family, friends, colleagues, and others who have supported and encouraged me on my journey so far. Without you, I wouldn't be where I am today. I am truly grateful for each one of you.

CONTENTS

INTRODUCTION

"Attitude is a choice. Happiness is a choice.
Optimism is a choice. Kindness is a choice. Giving is a
choice. Respect is a choice. Whatever choice you make
makes you. Choose wisely."

~ Roy T. Bennett, *The Light in the Heart* ~

How many choices will you make today? Some studies estimate adults on average make upwards of 35,000 choices *in a single day*. Mind-blowing, right? You make a huge percentage of these decisions without giving them much thought, which is only natural. But imagine what you could accomplish if a growing share of these choices were more consciously aligned to the dream life you want to live.

I'm twenty-eight years old as I write this, which means some of you are already wondering how a guy so young could be presumptuous enough to dish out advice on designing your dream life. Here's the thing: I haven't just designed my dream life, I'm *living* it right now, and I did it in less than a decade. I didn't have much of a head start, either. I had to make my dream life happen.

Making your dream life happen is like driving a car (or piloting a helicopter). Whatever your unique destination might be, you've got to know how to fuel, operate, and maintain your chosen vehicle if you want to get to your destination as quickly, efficiently, and safely as possible. I've written this book as a way of sharing my journey to date and the tools I've used to get me to this point. If my path inspires you and my methods help you along the way, then I've accomplished what I set out to do. Your journey will be different from mine, and the tools I've used may or may not be the right ones for you, and that's fine. Use what fits and gets results, disregard the rest, and keep searching for what's going to work best for you.

One thing I want to address from the outset is this: Don't wait! Start the journey to your dream life *now*. Don't wait for a tomorrow that may never come. Don't wake up years from now only to realize you never truly lived. Instead of putting your dream life off to some distant point in the future, figure out how to live your best life *today*. If all you do is *design* your dream life in your head, then it will remain exactly that—only a dream. I conducted a poll on Instagram (you can find me there at @alvaronunez) asking those who follow me what they wanted me to focus on in this book. Here are the results:

- Designing your dream life = 67%
- Clarifying vision and values = 17%
- Powerful routines and habits = 8%
- Turning obstacles into power = 17%

At the bottom of the poll, I added the text, "Or all of the above?" As you can probably guess, it takes all the above to craft a dream life. If what you want is to not just design but also *achieve* your dream life, then it's going to take real work and relentless focus, plain and simple. There are no shortcuts, and there is no free lunch. Are you willing to do whatever it takes to level up and make your dreams come true?

The good news is there are all kinds of tools out there to help you get your vehicle moving to a life like no other. Yes, you'll be working harder than ever to make it happen, but with the right tools and methods you'll also be working *smarter*, which is what can accelerate your momentum along the path toward your dream life. Each time you level up, take a moment to celebrate and then plan how you'll reach the next level.

Here's a preview of some of the essential tools that have gone into my own dream life journey:

VISION

What does your dream life look like? This is the most basic building block of all. Without a well-defined vision, you're dead in the water. If you don't envision it clearly, you won't be able to achieve it. I keep my vision front-and-center by going over it every day. I read it, I listen to an audio recording of myself speaking it, I look at photos that represent it, and I visualize it in my mind while activating all my senses. When you make your vision a daily multi-sensory experience, you'll accelerate your path toward it.

MY WHY

Closely related to vision, this one is more about *why* you want what you want, what you're going to do when you achieve your vision, what legacy you want to leave behind in the world, what you want to be known and remembered for, and so on. These can be strong motivators for leveling up.

THE WHEEL OF LIFE

The wheel has seven areas (career, social, family, intellectual, physical, spiritual, and financial) and serves as a framework to help you maintain forward momentum in all areas of your life. I use it to make sure I don't find myself way out of balance because I'm ignoring or not focusing enough on one or more areas of the wheel. The wheel of life is like a bicycle wheel with its spokes. Take out one of the spokes and slowly the wheel will begin to lose its shape, malfunction, and eventually become broken beyond repair. All the spokes need to be cultivated and carefully tended to achieve your dream life.

MAIN VALUES

What are the characteristics and behaviors you want to hold and maintain as you level up to your dream life? The *law of attraction* is important to keep in mind as you define your values because you'll get what you give. Live your life with good values and you'll find those good things will come back to you as well. Among my own main values are the following:

- Honesty
- Loyalty
- Passion
- Humility
- Empathy
- Empowerment

MINDSET

It's vital to cultivate one or even several mindsets that serve to propel you forward. This can include a growth mindset, the beast mentality, or others to help energize you and keep moving in the right direction, which is always toward your vision.

GOAL SETTING

You might be tempted to think goals are somehow outdated or blasé, but setting goals is absolutely an engine that can drive you in the right direction. There will be short-term goals and long-term goals. Some goals will be small, some will be massive. What they all have in common is propelling you forward and leveling up toward your destination.

HABITS AND ROUTINES

Achieving your dream life as quickly as possible can't happen if you don't cultivate the kinds of habits and routines that can get you there. This is where both time management and staying organized can make a huge difference on your journey. But there's more to it than that. There are many different practices you can adopt to keep yourself moving in the right direction, and when you turn these practices into habits and stack them into your daily routines to become second nature, you'll level up faster than ever and wonder how you ever got along without them!

WORDS OF TOUGHNESS

What are the words that capture *how* you're going to pursue your vision? What personal qualities will you need to embody if you're going to make your dreams come true? I call these *words of toughness*, and here are just a few examples that have been important in my life:

- **Resilience:** Most people will not experience a smooth ride to their dream life destination. There will be all kinds of challenges and obstacles along the way, some minor and some major. Resilience is about reframing setbacks into springboards. I've had to confront some very serious challenges in my journey, which you'll learn about in this book.

- **Focus:** Your focus must be constantly maintained, and it's also got to be strategic. Learn to be constantly vigilant so you'll see opportunities and make the most strategic move possible, both in-the-moment and in the bigger picture.

- **Relentless:** If you're serious about fulfilling your vision, then you must be relentless in pursuing it. Become relentless about living out your core values. Become relentless in setting goals and establishing good habits and effective routines. Becoming relentless turbocharges your progress.

While none of the individual pieces listed above are anything new, the unique combination and how I use them is the result of having tried all sorts of different methods, tools, and strategies. I've become truly passionate about continuous self-improvement and have invested a lot of time into studying countless resources. What's contained in this book is what has stuck from all that exploring because it helped me get the results I wanted.

My journey is far from over, and I'm incredibly humbled and excited to see where I go from here. The possibilities are endless for all of us, and we're all free to keep dreaming and envisioning our paths through life. What about you? Where are you at on life's journey? Have you envisioned and manifested your dream life? Do you want to get serious about *achieving* your dream life? Are you ready to become the hero of your own story and level up? If the answer is *yes*, and I sincerely hope it is, then this book is for you.

I can't and won't tell you what specific things should go into designing and achieving *your* dream life. What I can share with you is what has worked for me in hopes my story will inspire and empower you to go for it. All I ask is that you try the suggestions contained in this book to see if they can also work for you. And remember, there is no better time to start than right now, so don't wait.

Now, let's get rolling!

PART I

1

A CROSSROADS DECISION

"You are now at a crossroads. This is your opportunity to make the most important decision you will ever make. Forget your past. Who are you now? Who have you decided to become? Make this decision consciously. Make it carefully. Make it powerfully. Then act upon it."

~ Tony Robbins ~

I'm in the middle of a tennis match and the score is tied. As a fifteen-year-old, I've trained my way up to this moment—to compete and reach the finals of a prestigious national tournament. Determined to become a professional tennis player, every point counts, and the pressure during the match is high. Waiting for my opponent to make his next serve, out of the corner of my eye I notice my mother suddenly rise from her seat in the bleachers. There's a man leading her away from the match. I have no idea what's happening, but my concentration slips. I fail to return my opponent's serve, and then fail to return the next one as well. Then I see someone whispering to the referee, who immediately halts the match. I am escorted off the court in a rush to where my mother is waiting for me. She is as pale as a ghost, and I realize something is very wrong. I am told my father, who was over in the western part of the country on business, is in the hospital. He had a heart attack and is in a coma. Within minutes we are on the road, racing the nearly three hours it would take to reach the hospital.

* * * * *

That was the beginning of finding myself at the first major crossroads in my life—not an easy thing to confront as a teenager, especially as I went on to find out what had been happening behind the scenes I didn't even know about.

I was born and raised in Madrid, Spain. My father achieved great success as an architect and real estate developer at a young age. From his first marriage he had three children, and from his second marriage to my mother two more children, including me and my younger sister. These siblings from my father's previous marriage were all at least a decade older than me. There were my idols as a young child. Both of my older brothers had become professional racecar drivers, and one of them even competed at the highest class of international formula racing. Naturally, I was very inspired by them and wanted to follow in their footsteps.

My parents steered me into a variety of different sports. They believed strongly in both the physical and mental benefits of sports, including martial arts. I participated in basketball, tennis, judo, and soccer (as you can imagine, every kid growing up in Spain plays soccer). My father set a good example of always striving to be the best at anything he did, and I naturally did the same thing. As I got older, I became more focused on just two of these activities: tennis and Judo. Being involved in tennis and Judo wasn't just about doing them, it was about becoming as good as possible at them, not settling for anything less than being the best. What activities did you do when you were growing up? Did any of them "stick" and become something you continued to do as an adult?

By the time I reached high school age, I was good enough at tennis that everyone around me was saying I could pursue becoming a professional tennis player. I had been trained in some of the best tennis academies by the most accomplished coaches. I also achieved black-belt status in Judo when I was sixteen but had to stop at that point because there was too much risk of even small injuries hurting my tennis career. There also weren't the same kinds of professional opportunities in Judo as there were in tennis. Tennis became my full-time focus. For the last couple years of my secondary education, I attended a high school in Madrid that only enrolled elite athletes from all sports who wanted to become professional athletes. This was a school that produced world-class athletes, including classmates that became world champions such as Carolina Marin in badminton, Cristian Toro in canoeing an kayaking, Carlos Sainz in Formula 1 racing, and John Rahm in golf, among others.

The kind of physical and mental discipline it takes to become good enough in any sport to even consider trying to take it to the professional level served me well in all areas of my life. I was getting good grades thanks in part to the time management skills you've got to have when balancing academic studies with the demands of pro-track tennis while wanting to excel in both. It was a lot of pressure, and there were times when I hated tennis. But I was so consumed with it and my studies that I didn't have time for much else. I was shy and awkward socially, so I didn't have many friends to hang out with (or time for it, either). A bad temper and a lot of negative energy sometimes came out because of all this.

5

If anyone had looked at me through the lens of the Wheel of Life, they would have seen how out of whack it was. I was so focused on the career and physical spokes of the wheel I was completely ignoring the social and spiritual aspects. And while I had some focus on the family and intellectual areas, the financial aspect of life simply wasn't something I ever thought about at all. I grew up in a very comfortable, affluent family thanks to my father's successful career.

From the moment my father had his first heart attack, everything began to fall apart. Remember the global financial crisis of 2008? It's deceptive to call it a specific year because people think it happened in 2008. No, that's just when it started. The effects of that worldwide economic downturn lasted for years. My father was highly leveraged across multiple international real estate development projects and his whole professional career started to unravel when the financial crisis hit. With more than a thousand employees in business operations in Spain, Portugal, Brazil, and elsewhere, he tried desperately to hold it all together and keep things going, but everything crashed and burned. The stress of it all, combined with a less than healthy lifestyle, is what caused his heart attack. It is also what opened my eyes to the fact my family had basically lost everything.

All these things happening at once forced me to look differently at my life and what direction it would take. This was a lot for a teenager to deal with. I was at a crossroads, though I didn't think of it in those terms at the time. All I knew is I was suddenly seeing things differently than I had before. This crisis served as a huge reality check for me. My father did come out of his coma and was returned home, but the doctors told him he had to avoid stress as much as possible. But stress was exactly what came his way in full force with financial ruin. He tried to salvage what he could of his business, but even that proved too much and a few months later he had another heart attack and coma. The doctors did what they could with two different surgeries, but my father's heart was only operating at around 19 percent capacity. He either had to stop or he would kill himself. After that he went through a time where he was very withdrawn, isolated, and severely depressed.

Meanwhile, I had to figure out what direction my own life would take. Pursuing a professional tennis career suddenly looked a lot less attractive. I had seen people a few years older than me trying to go pro, only to be sidelined by an injury. I also had to consider my family's financial situation. Things were desperate. There were even times when we didn't have hot water at home. It really hit home for me when I looked realistically at trying to become a pro tennis player. There is no guarantee you'll achieve success and while I was good enough, it's not like I was a total superstar. Just as important, making the effort means investing a lot of money into professional coaches and traveling, which was something my family now couldn't do.

Should I just try to get a job of some kind to help provide for my family? The youth unemployment rate in Spain in the wake of the global financial crisis was insanely high, rising above 40 percent and higher. When school let out and summer vacation started, I worked twelve hours a day giving tennis lessons to anyone and everyone who could pay for them. It made sense to leverage my skills and abilities in this way. Then I realized if I really wanted to help my family and myself, I needed to get out of Spain. Everywhere I looked I saw young people who were just going through the motions. The economy was a wreck and everyone my age seemed to lack direction. They were settling for a very mediocre existence. So many people in Spain seemed to be small-minded and lacked ambition. I didn't want that to happen to me. I needed to get out. But how?

As the end of high school approached, going to college outside of Spain seemed like the right route to take. But where? I did have a friend, a fellow tennis player, who was a few years older than me, and he had leveraged tennis into a scholarship to attend university at an Oregon school in United States. He even offered to put me in touch with the guy who helped guide him in making it happen. After all, what better place to make a new start than the US, the place where people chase the American dream. My father was disappointed I might give up on the professional tennis track, but luckily my mother was very supportive of this new idea. She had to take on additional work to support the family, and I wanted to be sure I could make it on my own.

AT THE CROSSROADS: A VISION IS BORN

I was filled with excitement at the possibilities of using tennis to get myself a solid education and set myself up for a successful professional career. I allowed myself to dream big. I could see myself driving a white convertible Audi, living in a luxurious beach-side home in Miami with spectacular ocean views. Was it a teenager's simple vision of the American dream? Yes, it was, but it was also very energizing! While the decision to pursue a tennis scholarship to attend college in the US was the best strategic decision possible, it was what I saw in my head as my version of the American dream that gave me the energy and forward momentum to go for it. It was a new vision for me, and I was ready to make it happen.

Have you ever experienced finding yourself at a crossroads in your life? Maybe you've experienced it several times. Maybe you're at a crossroads right now in your life that has forced you to pause and reconsider your path forward. What should you do next? There are all kinds of factors to consider, but what helped me the most when I was at this first big crossroads in my own life was not just being strategic, but also letting myself dream big, and then taking action to make the dream a reality. *You can do the same.* Take a moment now to **write down 3–5 elements of your dream life** as if you were living it right now. This is the beginning of designing the dream life you're going to achieve. It's important to write it all down, whether on paper or on your phone, because *what you write, you invite.* This doesn't mean it will be easy to level up to your dream life. It wasn't easy for me, as you'll soon find out. Next stop, America!

2

MINDSET RESET

"It takes a different mindset to be successful in anything; that's why there's not a lot of super successful people, because there's guys I know who may be ten times more talented than me, but they don't work as hard."

~ Rico Love ~

Making the decision to leverage tennis into a college education in the US felt good, but there were a lot of details that had to come together to figure out what school would take me. It had to be a place that would give me a full scholarship, and it also had to be willing to work with my lack of English-speaking abilities. My parents hadn't emphasized learning English during my schooling because they figured everyone learns English along the way, so instead I had focused on learning German.

There were several good NCAA (National Collegiate Athletic Association) Division I schools with great tennis teams offering me scholarships that would have covered 85 or 90 percent of the total cost to attend, and I probably would have been their number-three or number-four player. But even that 10 or 15 percent of the cost not covered by scholarships was impossible for me given my family's new financial reality. It had to be a place that would cover 100 percent of the cost to attend. For me, that ended up being Western New Mexico University, located in Silver City, New Mexico. Well, at least there must be some Spanish speakers in New Mexico, right?

Keep in mind, when I was dreaming of going to the US and getting a college education, my vision of the American Dream was being an entrepreneur in the fast-paced city life of Miami. I'd be running my own company, driving around in my white convertible Audi, enjoying the views from my ocean-front apartment. As I thought about what college in the US would be like, I envisioned being around all these people my age who were also studying hard to achieve their own versions of the American Dream. I envisioned big classes, deep conversations with professors, lively parties, and all sorts of excitement. What I encountered was a far cry from the vision I had in my head.

Arriving to Silver City was the first rude awakening. After growing up in a thriving metropolis like Madrid with its more than 6.5 million population, I felt like I had been literally dropped into the middle of nowhere. Silver City was (and still is), a dry, dusty town with a population of only 10,000 people. There is not much of anything to do in this place. You must drive long distances to get to anything fun or exciting. Western New Mexico University (WMNU) is a public university with a grand total of 3,500 students.

The only bright spot I could see in all this was that as a Division II school, I could potentially be their star player. Their team had in fact won many consecutive championships and made it to nationals, so they did have a strong tennis team, as well as an excellent tennis coach who had a solid history of success. Unfortunately, this coach who had amazing plans for me, left WNMU just before I arrived! He was offered a head coach position at a Division I school in Las Vegas and took it. He wanted me to go with him, but he couldn't work out the full scholarship I needed. I had to stay put at least for a year.

I felt very out of place when I arrived to campus. Most of the athletic types were involved with the football team. I couldn't speak much English at all. As a result, I was quite introverted and found myself just observing everything around me rather than participating in anything. What I observed wasn't making me feel any better about being there. Part of why I left Spain was because everywhere I looked, young people my age lacked vision, direction, and ambition. They seemed small-minded and content to settle for mediocrity. My vision of college in the US didn't include being surrounded by people like that, and yet it's exactly what I was encountering here. So many of the students seemed like they were there to just party rather than educate themselves into a career or a future. They lacked vision. They did the minimum work needed to hopefully pass a class so they could get back to getting drunk. This was not what I wanted.

How could I make sure I wouldn't end up like all these people around me just going through the motions of school? I did a quick Google search: *How to keep my dreams alive.* One of the things that came up was something called a vision board. So, I created one. Was it simple? Yes. It just had what I had previously dreamt of—a white Audi convertible, a lovely home with ocean views, and running my own company. This vision board, a physical representation of my dreams, was just what I needed. It became a very real focal point serving as a constant reminder of the dream I wanted to achieve and motivator to level up.

Something else I realized quickly was that while a full scholarship would cover all the costs of attending WNMU,

I still needed money for just regular expenses of day-to-day living. I needed a job of some kind. I went to the career center and asked about what jobs were available on campus. The only opening they had was in the maintenance department. I took it because I didn't really have any other options. This job included mowing lawns and picking up trash. The irony was that the area where I worked was right around the tennis courts, which were also near the student dormitories. Here I was, the guy who was supposed to become the school's star tennis player, picking up trash around the tennis courts.

More times than I care to remember, students passing by would call out to me, "Hey Alvaro, what did you do wrong?"

The first time this happened, I must have had a puzzled expression on my face as I replied, "Nothing. Why?"

You see, my fellow students just assumed the only reason someone would be picking up trash around campus was as a punishment for something wrong. You could practically see the light bulb going off in their heads when they realized this was my *job*.

In short, I was feeling disappointed in just about every aspect of my situation because it was such a far cry from my vision. I rationalized it, however, as just being a starting point. My plan was to suffer only one year at this school. I figured if I could make a strong showing in everything my first year, both academically and in tennis, then I could transfer to a much bigger school in a much better location.

I began to strategically focus on how I could become a big fish in this small pond to facilitate getting me out of it. Being an introverted observer became my superpower. The school was small enough that I could begin to identify who were the few people who made things happen, who were in positions that could help propel me forward. I began forming strategic relationships with specific individuals who I thought could be of use to me. Every conversation I had was a calculated move on my part. As a keen observer, I would identify who was at the top in each setting and then I would set my sights on beating that person, whether it was on the tennis courts or in the classroom. I would fight my way to the top and then use it as a launching pad to get the heck out of there.

Then I broke my foot.

I had previously gone to the new tennis coach and asked him what I needed to do to become the top player not just of this team but in the whole country. He basically said I needed to train harder and smarter than everyone else and make it my top priority. He was right, of course. I knew I didn't have the raw talent to be the top player and become captain of the team, but I knew I could train harder than anyone else and make it happen. I would show up an hour early to do my own training, then go on to do the training with the rest of the team. The problem is I didn't quite hear *all* of what he said. I heard "train harder" and went for it. What I failed to hear was the word "smarter." I was overtraining for sure, and at first it was achieving the desired effect, but I wasn't being smart about it, so it also took a toll on my body. I was experiencing some pain in my right foot, which turned out to be a stress fracture, though I didn't know it at the time. All I knew was I had to keep training and performing as hard as I could.

I do give that new coach credit for helping me identify my path forward, but there was something weird about him I couldn't put my finger on. Turns out he had a long history as an abuser and the university quietly let him go just a couple months into the school year. Now the tennis team was without a head coach. The team needed leadership and direction, and it was my plan to provide it through the example of hard work.

The time came for our first off-season scrimmage match, and I knew this was where I needed to prove myself as someone with the drive to become the number-one player on the team. During my first match, as I was sprinting toward the net, there was an audible *crack*, which was the snapping of a bone in my right foot. I went down hard, and the pain was unbearable. I couldn't put any pressure on the foot at all. I couldn't even walk. I would be riding the bench for three months instead of rising to the top.

It felt like everything had completely unraveled for me. Here I was stuck in the middle of nowhere at a small school, no car to ever escape campus, and now not only without the original coach who helped get me to the US, but without any coach at all. This broken foot meant I would end up missing the whole first season of serious game play. So, there I was, still picking up trash around the tennis courts in my maintenance job, only now with the added insult of doing it while hobbling along on crutches. On top of all this, the university was going to cancel my scholarship! How could the school justify a full tennis scholarship when I couldn't even play? I was beginning to slip into a completely negative mental state full of bitterness and anger at my situation. I was deeply disappointed and frustrated.

I called up the coach who had gone to Las Vegas, hoping he could somehow bring me to his school. He said it would simply be impossible. There was no way he could take a tennis player from a small Division II school who wasn't even playing matches and bring him to a Division I school on any kind of scholarship. He said what I needed to do was first heal myself, then get back into the game and prove myself.

Was this what I wanted to hear? No, but it was what I needed to hear. It made me stop and ask myself, "At the very moment I needed peak performance to prove myself, why did my foot break?" It woke me up and made me realize I didn't just need to *physically* heal myself, I also needed to *mentally* heal myself. It was another kind of crossroads moment that made me see things differently. If I was going to become the hero of my own story and succeed at turning these obstacles into superpowers, I needed a *mindset reset*. Here's how it looked for me:

KEEPING YOUR VISION AND YOUR WHY FRONT-AND-CENTER

I was speaking with my younger sister who was back in Spain. She was in tears because of how difficult the family environment and financial situation had become. With my father severely depressed and my mother trying to hold it all together and provide for the family, there wasn't even hot water in the house, and she feared the electricity would be shut off. This was an important moment to me. It was a reminder that part of my vision or my "why" was to become successful so I would be able to help my family. How could I allow myself to be self-absorbed in my own negativity when my family back in Spain was truly suffering? I couldn't let my present circumstances distract me from my vision, or my "why" of helping my family.

IDENTIFYING CORE VALUES

Something I've done in recent years is to reflect on my core values. I've identified the ones that have been most important to me over the years and review them frequently to remind myself of how important they are to achieving success. Below are the ones that bubbled up to the surface as I think back to this mindset reset time in my life:

- **Honesty:** I wasn't being honest with myself about the person I was becoming. I was allowing myself to become increasingly negative and resentful, and it wasn't doing me any favors.

- **Loyalty:** I wasn't being loyal to anything or anyone beyond myself. Becoming too self-centered and selfish is simply not the kind of energy that attracts good things to you, and I was learning this the hard way.
- **Humility:** I embraced the humility of my situation. Limping around on crutches picking up trash around the tennis courts when you're supposed to be the star player is a very humbling situation. When I looked around at some of the adult workers in the maintenance department, I stopped seeing them as being stuck in a dead-end menial job. I began to see them as people working hard to feed their families, as people who found dignity in their job and who took pride in doing their work well. For them, these maintenance jobs were their livelihood. Who was I to feel anything but grateful for the opportunity to earn some much-needed money?
- **Empathy:** I wasn't being empathetic to anyone around me. I was treating everyone as if they were little more than a steppingstone to where I wanted to be, and no one likes to be stepped on. Doing so will likely come back to bite you in some way. Karma is like that.

EFFECTIVE HABITS

It's hard to fulfill your vision and make your dreams come true without having plenty of good habits to help you along the way.

- **Adding Value:** When you're in a tennis match, the whole point is to win by beating your opponent, so it's only natural I would have that mindset of leveling up by beating others in whatever the game was, whether tennis or academics. In a tennis match you might go on the offensive with aggressive attacks to beat your opponent. But then I thought about everything I learned in Judo. The point in Judo isn't to aggressively attack your opponent to beat them, it's to avoid being defeated by someone attacking you. In other words, trying to become a big fish in a small pond by beating people wasn't the smart play. The smarter play was to become a big fish in a small pond by finding opportunities to bring value to the community, not by beating people down to win. If the focus is to add value to the community, then everybody wins.

When was the last time you realized *you* needed a mindset reset? Did you embrace it, or did you avoid it? Avoiding it is the easy way out. Embracing it means putting in the work to make it happen. A mindset reset is a beautiful thing, but it doesn't feel that way at first. Why? Because you realize how you have failed. Not everyone has the self-awareness or desire to get real with themselves and recognize their own role in shaping whatever circumstances they are in. I could just as easily have allowed myself to get stuck in self-pity at everything that seemed to be going wrong for me. I could have let myself adopt a victim mentality where all these bad things were happening *to* me without seeing how I was part of the problem. But I also knew deep down I had to be honest with myself if was going to turn these obstacles into superpowers.

I did not know about things like the *law of attraction* at this point in my life. But there was something inside me that intuitively knew I needed to change my mental state if I wanted to change how things were going around me. The most powerful motivator for me during this time was the "why" behind my vision, a significant element of which has always been to help my family. What's *your* why? Take a few minutes now to think about and **write down 3 reasons *why***

you want to achieve your dream life. Will it require a mindset reset? If so, embrace it! If you're willing to embrace the need for a mindset reset, great things can happen, just like they did for me, which is what you'll discover in the next chapter.

3

THE PIVOT TO POSITIVITY

"In every day, there are 1,440 minutes. That means we have 1,440 daily opportunities to make a positive impact."

~ Les Brown ~

When I reached the end of my very rough freshman year at the university, it felt great to put it squarely in the rearview mirror. It was over. I had my mindset reset. Now it was time for the real work to begin. The first item on my to-do list was to figure out how I was going to pay tuition if I lost my tennis scholarship. It was a 100% full-ride scholarship, so I had to get creative.

First off, I kept my maintenance job. It was important to me to embrace it now that I had shifted my mindset from feeling humiliated by it to feeling humbly grateful for having any job at all. Then I started looking around for whatever scholarships I could apply for. I went to every department on campus to ask about what support they were offering. I started working with the student government to see what opportunities I might be able to connect with through them.

I also once again found myself leveraging my tennis skills into income by coaching tennis on the side while also exploring reducing my housing cost by becoming a paid resident assistant or living off-campus with roommates to have more affordable rent. The combination of being both creative and persistent helped me figure it out.

After making sure my foot was properly healed, I took my renewed sense of determination to move forward and applied it to everything. I started my maintenance work around 4:30am. Then I'd go do my own workout at the gym at 5:30am. Then, when the rest of the tennis team showed up at 6:00am for training, I joined them for that as well. Why? I knew I wasn't the most talented tennis player on the team in terms of raw skill and natural ability. But the coach had previously told me I could still be the top player on the team if I trained harder and smarter than everyone else. Even if I wasn't the star tennis player, I could be the one in the better shape—and I was going to do it right this time to avoid any injuries (you know, *like breaking my foot*). I was going to become the strongest possible version of myself.

What's interesting is what happened when the rest of the tennis team saw this determination. Before long, quite a few others also started showing up early to do extra training. Was there a competitive factor at play here? Yes, of course there was. But there was also a team mentality. We didn't want to just become better as individuals, we wanted to become better for the sake of the team. As the new tennis coach watched me working harder than everyone else, as well as how my example got others to do the same, he would eventually name me captain of the tennis team. Was I the best player on the team? No, but what the coach saw leadership qualities in me just as important as raw talent or skill at playing the sport.

When I was approaching the end of the year, everything was moving along in all the right directions. I still wanted to transfer to a different college in a better environment, and I applied to quite a few. I was accepted into some great schools that offered me good scholarships. The tennis team had made it to nationals that spring, and during the tournament I built some great relationships with coaches at other schools. I could have transferred to any number of colleges, but ultimately I decided to stay put in Silver City. I realized how much of a positive impact it was having on me, and I also realized I wasn't done making my own positive contributions.

You see, during my freshman year I didn't have the right mindset. I felt so out of place and introverted. I had decided to improve myself, but it was out of a very selfish motivation because of how negative I was feeling about everything. I didn't want to have a positive impact on the community around me, I just wanted to do whatever I could to get ahead. It was the wrong approach, and I only ended up hurting myself. I remember saying to myself, "Alvaro, what are you doing? Why have you allowed yourself to become so negative and selfish?" The moment I asked myself those questions, I realized I could choose a different path.

The law of attraction works on both the good and the bad. If what you put out in the world is selfishness and negativity, that's what you'll get back. The mindset reset I went through meant I had put all that aside to start bringing real value to everything and everyone around me, not just for myself but for the team, for the campus community, and beyond. And when I started putting all that positivity out in the world around me, it came back to me many times over! As retired world-champion gymnast Mary Lou Retton puts it, "Optimism is a happiness magnet. If you stay positive, good things and good people will be drawn to you."

Instead of asking how I could improve myself or how I could get ahead, it became increasingly important to ask how many lives could I touch in a positive, empowering way?

How much of a positive impact can I have on the different communities I'm in? When you start thinking and behaving from this kind of positive perspective, it feels great! In fact, it can become addictive, but in a good way. It makes you want to do more of it, and by doing more of it, then you attract even more goodness to yourself.

I was leaning into the entrepreneurial content in my business and marketing studies, which led to getting involved in all sorts of things. I had the opportunity to serve as president of the campus chapter of the Delta Mu Delta International Honor Society in Business. I also founded and served as president of the campus Marketing Club. It brought together students from all disciplines who wanted hands-on learning experiences focused on marketing. The club worked with businesses in the local community to develop marketing strategies and implement them as part of their overall business plan. I also got involved as a senator in the student government (the Associated Students of Western New Mexico University). Meanwhile, I was also keeping up with my studies and getting good grades.

The result of all this work was being chosen as Valedictorian of the Class of 2015. I was also inducted into the school's Student Hall of Fame (one of only four students inducted that year). Here's how it is described on the school's website:

> The Hall of Fame is reserved for those students who have demonstrated integrity and achievement through leadership activities, community involvement, participation in campus life, and scholarship while attending Western New Mexico University. As a result of their exceptional impact on the campus community, these student leaders distinguish themselves from many other outstanding students.

I was both humbled and proud of being selected. As Valedictorian I had the opportunity to give a goodbye speech at the graduation ceremony, but what happened after my speech was completely unexpected. When the President went to the podium he said, "Thank you, Alvaro, for your inspiring speech, but don't be too quick to say goodbye. I think we may be seeing Alvaro around campus for a while yet."

I had no idea what he was talking about because I was planning on getting away from Silver City as soon as I could after graduation. When the ceremony was over, the President asked me to stop by his office later in the day. When I went to see him, I still didn't have a clue as to what was going on or why he wanted to see me.

In his office, the President got right down to business. He said, "Alvaro, the board of directors has authorized a significant one-time spend on marketing. We've created a brand-new Marketing Coordinator position to oversee all campus marketing initiatives, and we want *you* to take the job."

I was stunned. I didn't know what to make of this spontaneous job offer. My mind was racing. I had already been making the shift toward looking for marketing jobs and graduate school programs in southern Florida because my vision was to end up in Miami. But now here was this incredible opportunity literally being handed to me. But it also meant staying in Silver City, New Mexico, the place I had been trying to leave ever since I arrived! I was beginning to wonder if I'd *ever* get out of Silver City. Every time I tried to leave, something happened to make me stay, and this was no exception. All I could manage was, "I don't know what to say."

While the President explained more about what the job would involve, my rational mind kicked in and I could see what an incredible opportunity this was. I could gain some much-needed marketing experience with an employer I knew in a place where everyone knew me, and which now felt very familiar to me. And the salary that came with the position was way more than most new graduates could hope for. It made total sense to accept the position, even though it would keep me more distant from Miami than I wanted to be at the time.

Then I said, "But I've already sold all my furniture and gave up my housing." After all, as far as I was concerned, I was leaving Silver City within a couple days and never coming back.

"Alvaro don't worry about any of that," the president said, "we'll cover it. All you need to do is say *yes*."

I hesitated for a moment, but when I opened my mouth, I heard myself say, "Yes!"

Logistically, what happens to an international college student on an education visa is that after you graduate, you basically have a year to figure out your next move or you're out of the country. One option is what I did called OPT status, which stands for Optional Practical Training. The OPT work permit is a temporary employment provision allowing graduating international students to work for one year as a kind of extension of the student visa. After the one-year OPT, then the choices are extending the student visa further to cover graduate school or applying for a work visa by securing a job with an employer willing to sponsor it. In my mind, it was a no-brainer to commit to one more year in Silver City as an employee of the university, and at the end of the OPT year decide where to go next.

VALUES TO LIVE BY

Throughout these years at college, core values were coming into view that would remain important to me in the years ahead, including the following:

Hard Work: One of the biggest learning points through the final three years of my undergraduate studies has to do with my approach to work, meaning my work ethic. Remember in the previous chapter how my tennis coach had told me that the path to becoming the best player was to train harder and smarter than everyone else? I embraced the "train harder" part but not the "smarter" part of the equation and ended up with a broken foot. You know how people say *work smarter, not harder?* That's all well and good, but if you really want to accelerate your path forward toward your vision, then my recommended approach is to work *both* smarter *and* harder! It was important to remain humble, passionate, and empowering of others, and I also had to be willing to work both smarter and harder than ever to achieve not only greater personal development for its own sake, but also to make a real and positive impact on the community. And it really paid off! You've got to ask yourself, are you willing to put that effort in? Are you willing to work both smarter and harder to level up to your vision?

Loyalty: Are you being *loyal* to your vision? How this looks as it plays out might not always seem like you're moving closer to your vision. After all, I wasn't getting any nearer to Miami by staying in Silver City! It was the right move to make considering the practical benefits I'd get that would then facilitate my next move. Loyalty is one of my most important values. In this case, it wasn't just being loyal to myself and my vision, but also being loyal to the university where I had grown so much during my time as a student there. For all these reasons, investing in another year in Silver City seemed like the right way to be both loyal to the university and be rewarded with something in return that would help me.

Deciding what your main values will be as you level up to your dream life is an essential step of the process. Take some time now to **write down 5 main values** you want to live by, keeping in mind the law of attraction because what you put out in the world is what you'll get back!

As the end of my OPT year approached, I applied to a bunch of different graduate schools in Florida. I was accepted into many of them, but once again the finances. There really aren't any scholarships for international students to attend graduate school the way there are for undergraduate studies. What I needed was a good GA (Graduate Assistant) position that would cover all the costs of graduate school. I needed to stand out as much as possible from all the other applicants, so I chose to focus on the marketing angle since I was just coming off a year of incredible practical experience leading the marketing department of a university. I was chosen for a GA position at two different schools, and the one I ended up choosing to attend was Lynn University in Boca Raton, Florida—one of the wealthiest zip codes in the country.

Behind this decision were several factors I considered. It was a small school, which meant I knew I could have the kind of positive campus community impact as I did at Western New Mexico University. They had one of the best tennis programs in the nation, which I knew would be important for me in terms of continuing to leverage my tennis skills into various opportunities. I could also see the student body was largely made up of wealthy international young people, which I knew could be an important asset for potential entrepreneurial opportunities. All in all, it seemed to be the obvious choice for me, so off I went. Next stop, South Florida!

4

A WHOLE NEW WORLD

"Try not to become a man of success.
Rather become a man of value."

~ Albert Einstein ~

I was twenty-two years old when I arrived in Boca Raton to attend Lynn University to get my MBA (Master of Business Administration) degree. The decision to land there was based on my assessment of the place and the school. What I discovered, however, was many times more than what I anticipated. It was the exact opposite of Silver City.

The Bloomberg Wealth Report tracks the 100 richest zip codes in the nation, and southern Florida is well-represented on the list, including Boca Raton. In fact, when I came to the area in 2016, Boca Raton topped the list of South Florida Business Journal's wealthiest zip codes list. I had never seen so many high-end luxury cars on the streets in one place—Ferrari, Porsche, Lamborghini—it seemed like *everyone* was driving around in cars I had only dreamed of. I didn't even have my own car when I came to Boca Raton. It was a far cry from Silver City, where people often drove broken-down cars in really rough shape.

As a small, private, expensive school, Lynn University was its own microcosm of wealth, especially the international students. I watched as students pulled up in those same luxury cars I was seeing around Boca Raton. They obviously came from wealthy families well-positioned here in the US or in their home countries. The university had positioned itself as the destination school for the international upper-class crowd. It wasn't hard to find out just how elite many of the students were. Some of them were the children of the richest families in their countries, or the children of former prime ministers and other positions of influence in the government. To me, it looked like the perfect network to explore business opportunities while extending my knowledge through continuing my education.

Boca Raton also has an impressive presence in the tennis world. Back in the 1970s the idea of the private tennis academy was born in Florida. Today, Florida is widely considered the tennis capital of the entire world. In fact, for a long time the USPTA (United States Professional Tennis Association) was headquartered in Boca Raton because so many of the best tennis academies were located there. If you've seen the movie *King Richard* starring Will Smith as Richard Williams, the father of pro tennis stars Serena and Venus Williams, they did much of their training at tennis academies in the area. In fact, quite a few of the top tennis players in the world have spent time training there. Tennis became another avenue to make inroads at various country clubs in the area and their members by offering up my skills in tennis to help those who wanted to improve their game.

I was also thinking ahead to what my next major move would be. After all, there would be a lot at stake in terms of whether I could stay in the US after finishing the degree as an international student. I'd be eligible to apply for another OPT (Optional Practical Training) where I would get a job and work for a year, and at the end of it either the company I'd be working for would decide to sponsor me in obtaining a work visa, or I'd have to come with a different plan.

One year, however, is not much time to prove yourself valuable enough to a company for them to go through hassles, headaches, and expense of sponsoring a person through work visa application process. I really wanted to stay in the US, so I needed to find the right job for an OPT. I was think-ing to myself, "Alvaro, you've got to prove yourself worthy and become indispensable to a company." Should I go for a large company? Right away the voice in my head said, "No way. You need to stand out, and that's going to be hard to do when you're lost in a whole sea of employees. The smart move would be a startup." This was an important strategic choice, and one that has helped me on more than one occa-sion. Standing out from the crowd is a great way to accelerate you on the path toward your vision.

Speaking of my vision, it always included being in Miami and now that I was so much closer to it physically, it made sense to spend time down there to explore possibilities. I got into the habit of taking the one-and-a-half-hour Tri-Rail train ride from Boca Raton to Miami as often as I could, bringing a bag of tennis balls and my other tennis equipment with me. I then went straight to the most expensive condominium buildings I could find that also had tennis courts, which were in South Beach. In the SoFi (South of Fifth) area of Miami were buildings like the Continuum, the Murano Grande, and the Murano at Portofino—the playground of the rich and famous.

At first, I would just sit and observe people on the courts. I looked the part of a professional tennis player, so most people didn't mind if I offered up some tips or advice. For example, one day there was a guy whose forehand was often sending the ball straight into the net. I said to him, "If you change your grip slightly in this way, open it up a little, and then follow-through, your forehand will be much better."

The man took my advice, and his forehand was immediately better. He came over to me and said, "Wow! Your advice really worked! Are you some kind of tennis pro or coach?"

After telling about my tennis experience, it was the perfect opportunity to say, "I'm giving lessons later today if you want one." The guy was all in, so we worked out a time he would come back and what lessons with me would cost.

It didn't take long to build up a portfolio of people I was coaching, and they were all well-connected and successful, which I knew just from the fact they could afford to live in one of these luxury buildings. They were also willing to pay whatever fee I quoted them for lessons, and these South Beach tennis trips became surprisingly lucrative.

Eventually, one of the people I was coaching put me in contact with a successful entrepreneur who was starting a powerful marketing-related business where I would be a good fit. The startup was all about helping small and medium-sized businesses get better marketing exposure to help them thrive, which was very aligned with my interests. It also had a great salary to start with as well. To top it all off, they even had an office in Boca Raton.

I was hired to be one of the company's leading marketing coordinators. Each one of us was responsible for 25–50 different business clients. Now I just had to figure out how to become indispensable to the company by being the best I could be at the job. I set my sights on becoming the Director of Operations, which just so happened to be my boss's job.

How could I bring something to the table none of the other marketing coordinators were doing? When I started looking into how I could handle taking on more clients, I realized the extent to which my colleagues weren't leveraging the systems and tools right there in front of them. This would be my opportunity to work both smarter and harder.

For example, the company had very robust CRM (customer relationship management) software, but my fellow marketing coordinators were only using it as a glorified rolodex for calling up clients when they needed to talk to them. This was a huge waste of potential. There were all sorts of things I could automate through the CRM (this was the working smarter part of the equation) but then I took it even further and developed my own system (the working harder part of the equation) for creating more follow-up touchpoints and upselling opportunities with clients all while utilizing the CRM to make it happen as smoothly and easily as possible. The result was me being able to quickly build much stronger relationships with clients (which is the whole purpose of CRM software to begin with) as well as increase my capacity to handle more clients. Instead of just fifty like most of the marketing coordinators, within a matter of weeks I was successfully managing 250 clients.

My boss was very impressed, but I decided to accelerate my path toward getting her job by making a bold move. I went to the owner of the company and made him an offer. I mentioned how I had seen him driving his son to tennis lessons, and I offered to coach his son once a week in exchange for him to sit down once a month with me for a mentoring session. He was impressed with me taking the initiative as well as my ambition in expressing my desire to work my way up into the Director of Operations position. He agreed to take me on, which immediately put me on the path to getting the position I wanted. After all, he was now invested in seeing me succeed. I was no longer just another employee, I was the employee in whom he was taking a personal interest, which meant his own reputation was now at stake. Within two months, I did in fact become the company's Director of Operations.

By the time I turned 23, I was literally living my dream! I was making a six-figure income, overseeing more than 100 employees, driving my white convertible Audi, and living in an apartment with views of the water. My original vision board was realized.

DREAMING BIG AND STAYING TRUE TO YOUR VISION

When I decided to really bring as much value to my employer as possible, it wasn't out of a motivation to beat my fellow employees. I was doing it because I could see it was my pathway forward toward my vision. My vision was simply bigger than what most of my colleagues apparently wanted. They were settling for their status quo, for whatever reason.

This was what I saw so often in Silver City as well, and it was something I wanted to avoid—getting comfortable, settling for the status quo, not striving for something much bigger. If people are happy with their regular nine-to-five life, more power to them. But how many of them *did* have a dream or vision for their life and then let it go? Once you give up on your dream and settle for less than your vision, you can easily become stuck there. And the longer you stay stuck there the harder it is to rekindle the flame of your vision and once again embark on the adventure of achieving it. This is when I started thinking of "being comfortable" as kryptonite—the one thing that could rob Superman of his superpowers.

Dreaming big is important. As Paul Coehlo puts it: "If you really think small, your life will be small. If you think big, your world will be big." You've got to have a big vision and stay focused on taking the steps to move you closer to it. Are you all in? If so, then jump right in with both feet, be relentless in working both smarter and harder to make it happen, bring as much value as you can to the table, and then watch the results start rolling in.

STAYING COMMITTED TO YOUR CORE VALUES

Below are some of the core values that surfaced during this time of my life that I remain deeply committed to today:

- **Adding Value:** Many people want to be successful, but as Einstein mentioned in the quote at the beginning of this chapter, instead of trying to become successful, just focus on being a person of value. When you are the person who adds value to every situation and everyone you meet, success will naturally follow.
- **Passion:** During my undergraduate studies, I discovered the passion I had for digital marketing. Throughout my MBA studies, I learned as much as I could from every resource I could put my hands on. I knew I didn't want to settle for just being average at a bunch of different things. I wanted to truly excel at something I was passionate about. If you can identify this one thing, then you've got to give it your all to become the very best you can be at it. This was a lesson I learned from my father, who was always driven to be the very best he could at anything he took on.
- **Continuous Improvement:** You can't ever stop and think you've made it. You've got to keep driving yourself to become better and better if you want to stand out and level up to your vision. And it's not about being better than other people, it's about continuously improving yourself so you're always becoming a better you.

34

If the dream life you want to achieve is ambitious, you'll need to be the very best version of yourself as possible. Take a moment now to **write down 5 things you know you need to improve about yourself**. After all, self-awareness and being honest with yourself will be critical to succeeding at leveling up. Of course, even when it feels like everything is on track and moving in the right direction, you must also be mentally prepared for all of it to blow up in your face at any moment, which is exactly what happened to me next.

5

WAKE-UP CALL

"The loss of a job may be the wake-up call needed
to redeem the fire of your genius."

~ Dan Miller ~

At first, I was totally excited about being promoted to Director of Operations, but then reality set in. I began to have serious doubts. I said to myself, "What in the world have I gotten myself into? Sure, I know a lot about marketing, but I don't know anything about managing people. This could be a real train wreck if I don't get up-to-speed." I was letting this voice of doubt get to me. I countered it by looking at what I could do to fill in these gaps in my knowledge on the fly as I figured out how to do my job as efficiently and effectively as possible.

A friend of mine who had recently graduated from Harvard was telling me about how much he had learned and the amazing contacts he made, mentioning how there were fast-track programs that would be perfect for me. I found an executive program at Harvard for those who had completed their master's degree and were in a significant executive position in a company. The Director of Operations at the marketing startup qualified, so I applied and was accepted. Luckily, the program was setup as a hybrid offering, which meant I could participate mostly remotely and only fly up to Boston when necessary.

This was an incredibly intense six months. I was obsessed with maintaining peak performance in my position at the startup, so I was already putting in thirteen-hour days at the office, from 7am to 8pm. How could I fit this Harvard executive program into a schedule like that? I had to start my day as early as possible. I would get up at 2:45am so I could be studying by 3am. After two-and-a-half hours of studying, I'd then drive to the gym for a quick workout and from there go directly to the office by 7am. I'd leave the office usually around 8pm, grab some dinner, and then go straight to bed around 9pm at night.

Sounds crazy, right? It was, but I'm also a firm believer in what David Goggins once said: "High achievement doesn't require inborn talent. It requires working your ass off. Period." You can, of course, overdo it. But I was determined to succeed in my position. It was the perfect OPT position to keep me in the country after finishing my MBA, complete the Harvard executive program, and possibly sponsor me through the work visa application.

What did these thirteen-hour days at the office involve? A lot of the time it was just about keeping up with what felt like a runaway freight train barreling down the tracks at 90 miles an hour. The company was growing so fast, sometimes systems put in place one day might very well be scrapped the next day for something else. The company could change directions on a dime, and I had to roll with wherever it was heading. The owners of the company were a couple of guys well known for their serial entrepreneurship. They'd start a company, grow it super-fast into something incredible, and then sell it off to the highest bidder.

In this kind of chaotic startup environment, the owners are the ones driving the train, plowing through any barriers standing in the way of what they envisioned for the company. This could leave quite a mess in its wake, and my job was often about picking up the broken pieces and putting them back together in some way so the whole operation could keep going. Of course, a lot of times those broken pieces were employees I was managing. It was a crash course in managing people, some of whom wondered how a guy as young as me could be the one in charge of such a large team.

Toward the end of the OPT, I began working with an immigration lawyer to apply for a work visa so I could remain in the US, and my employer was willing to sponsor me through the process. But then came the big wake-up call, and it was a rude awakening.

I did not get the work visa. In fact, my application wasn't even considered!

What many people don't realize is that less than 50% of work visa applications are accepted into the formal review process. Of the ones that do get the full review, an even smaller percentage of those end up obtaining a work visa. I didn't even make it past the first cut!

This was not a minor speed bump on my journey. It was like crashing head-on into a brick wall. It was literally game over. Without a work visa, I would have to leave the country. I was sorely disappointed with this turn of events. The thirteen-hour days at the office, the early morning studying, it was all focused on getting a work visa, and it didn't happen. Now what would I do?

My employer, of course, had no choice but to let me go. They needed a Director of Operations who was there on the ground, keeping the train on the tracks, and it couldn't be me because I would now have to leave the country.

When was the last time you put all your efforts into something, only to have it blow up in your face? Maybe you were putting 100% of your energy into a relationship but the other person decided to just walk away from it. Maybe you were giving 100% to perfecting your performance in a sport because you had set your sights on becoming a professional athlete, but then experience an injury that stopped you in your tracks. When I was on the professional tennis track, I saw this happen all too often to athletes with big dreams. Or maybe you were putting 100% into you career and it took a toll on your health in a way that stopped you from working at all, like what happened to my father. Each one of these scenarios is a serious wake-up call. Have you ever experienced one? Are you experiencing one right now in your life? This is when it's helpful to pause and reflect on what your Wheel of Life looks like.

THE WHEEL OF LIFE

The seven spokes in the Wheel of Life include career, social, family, intellectual, physical, spiritual, and financial. What happened to me in becoming the Director of Operations at the startup company was becoming so focused on my career that I literally ignored all the other spokes on the Wheel of Life. I was ignoring everything else, including friends and family, which means my wheel was completely out of balance.

Have you ever heard the phrase *don't put all your eggs in one basket*? This is exactly what I was doing with my career obsession. It's a dangerous thing to put all your eggs in one basket because if something happens to the basket, all the eggs are at risk of being broken and then you're left with nothing. No bicycle wheel can maintain its well-rounded shape with only one spoke. All the spokes need to be present, accounted for, and actively nurtured to maintain a well-rounded life. All the areas on the wheel are deeply intertwined. They all feed and support the whole.

Not having my work visa application even considered was like someone bumping into me and making me drop my basket of eggs. Watching the basket fall to the ground and seeing all the eggs shatter into a big mess became a major wake-up call.

After the initial wave of disappointment about the work visa, I could see very clearly how out of balance my life had become. It's never easy to look at yourself and realize you allowed yourself to put all your eggs in one basket and the mess you've now got to deal with. This is the wake-up call, and what you do next will determine whether your setback becomes something that breaks you or becomes a springboard to launch you into a new phase of your growth as a person. When you get your wake-up call, if all you do is hit the snooze button and go back to sleep, then you'll miss your chance to turn your setback into a springboard. One of the most important things you can and should do after getting a wake-up call is return to your vision.

If you're going to be intentional about lifestyle design, then you must do more than just visualize your dream life. Designing it means you've got to have a vehicle of some kind to help get you there, whether that's your own business, your job, or a special project. Whatever it may be, it's got to be something you're passionate about, because passion is the fuel that turbocharges your forward momentum toward your vision. Part of what I had to do after receiving my wake-up call was to reassess whether the vehicle I was using was the right one. Clearly, it was not. I needed to realign with my vision as I considered what to do next.

REALIGNING TO YOUR VISION

When I thought about my vision, it suddenly became clear how far I had strayed from it. My vision was to be an entrepreneur running my own company. Instead, by becoming obsessed with my job and what I could accomplish there, it was all wrong. Why was I putting in thirteen-hour days for anyone other than me? Working for someone else was never part of my vision unless it was a necessary steppingstone toward my vision, but I had become stuck in the position and let it consume me. It was like I was wearing blinders and couldn't see my vision anymore, until I got my wake-up call. Hard as it was to realize all this, I became truly grateful for my rude awakening. Now I could rekindle my vision and get back on track moving toward it.

The immediate question for me was, now what? I had to leave the country. Where should I go? Everyone was telling me I should go back to Spain. With my education and experience, I could easily get a great job, right? But my vision wasn't about slaving away for someone else. I needed to go someplace where I could make something beautiful and inspiring.

My mother has always been one of my biggest supporters, and I remembered how my vision included being able to support and help family when needed. My mother understood why I did not want to return to Spain and supported my decision not to go there. Instead, she suggested I come to the Dominican Republic where she and my father were now living and help her develop her real estate business. As soon as she mentioned it, I realized it was a no-brainer and exactly the right step to take because it was aligned with my vision. Take a few minutes to **write down 3 steps you could take to level up toward the vision of your dream life**. You just set four important goals! Now start working out what you must do to accomplish them. For me, I knew going to the DR was a great option. It was one of those moments of clarity where you just know in your heart it's the right thing to do.

Next stop, the Dominican Republic!

PART II

6

LEAP OF FAITH

"There are many talented people who haven't fulfilled their dreams because they overthought it, or they were too cautious and were unwilling to make the leap of faith."

~ James Cameron (filmmaker) ~

I arrived in the Dominican Republic in 2017 with mixed emotions. On one hand, I felt great. It was like having a big blank canvas in front of me, a blank slate to begin something new and different in my life. Making a fresh start in a new place is exciting! On the other hand, it can also come with some fears and anxieties. Those anxieties might come from within as well as from external sources. Everyone was telling me I should go back to Spain where I could easily land a great job. I was defying all that advice because it simply did not align with my vision. On the other hand, would I really be able to develop something significant in the DR? It felt like the only things I really had going for me were my own vision and determination, as well as the support of my mother.

What was happening here was an important shift in my life. Up until this point, the way I leveraged myself into all kinds of wonderful opportunities was through tennis, which you saw throughout Part I of this book. Many of the opportunities presented to me through tennis were ones that allowed me to develop my knowledge, experience, and true passion for marketing. Now the time had come to fully lean into marketing as the vehicle to accelerate progress toward my vision. From here forward, tennis would no longer be my primary point of leverage, but I remain deeply grateful for everything tennis did to get to this point in my life.

My mother had previously mentioned that one of the nicer properties she had recently sold in the Dominican Republic went to a client who was only going to use it once or twice a year as a vacation home. He asked my mother if she could arrange for it to be rented out to people looking for a place to stay in the DR when he wasn't using it. In the spirit of saying *yes* to everything because of how it can jumpstart opportunities, she agreed. She asked me to get involved in developing a way to effectively market the property to people who might want to rent it.

I was aware of the rise of Airbnb, which at that time was just beginning its international expansion, but it still had little presence in the Caribbean beyond a handful of listings. It occurred to us we could do something similar in the DR but focused on nicer properties and a more elite clientele. Why? Because I noticed most of the great waterfront properties were sitting empty most of the year! The owners lived elsewhere and only occasionally came to visit. And the travel agencies serving the more elite clients didn't have any of the DR's best properties listed in their portfolios. The opportunity was coming into focus, but I needed to find out if the property owners were interested in the idea.

I decided the best way to find out how people would react to the idea of allowing an agency to rent their property out when they weren't using it was to just go directly to those beautiful waterfront properties and start knocking on doors. I will admit I found this idea rather intimidating. The thought of walking up to a house and knocking on the door made me nervous.

There was voice inside my head saying, "This is a dumb idea. You're going to knock on the doors of strangers' homes? What are you going to say? You're going to look like an idiot." But I was determined to make a go of it, so I counteracted that pesky inner voice with preparation. I rehearsed what I would say. I thought through all the possible objections and had answers ready for them. When the day came to give it a try, I put on one of my best suits. Why? It's important to dress for success. When you look good, you feel better about yourself and make a better first impression on people. Even though I was still a little nervous, I also felt confident because I had prepared well and looked the part.

I went around knocking on doors of the best waterfront properties, and even though I encountered rejections, I was gaining more confidence through the repetitions. I'd ask whoever answered the door (usually a housekeeper or groundskeeper) if the owner was home, and the answer was often no. Then I'd explain how I might have someone interested in renting the home if I could just talk to the owner. Sometimes the person would call the owner on the spot and let me speak with them. Other times I'd give them my business card so they could pass my contact information on to them.

When I did get to speak with the owners, most of them were interested by the idea. Then I could set a follow-up meeting and provide examples of how I would show their property online. As a marketer, I knew the key to success with this idea was all about presentation, including gorgeous professional-grade photographs and compelling descriptions highlighting the luxurious aspects of the home. We started with a few properties, posting them everywhere we could. The real challenge was to figure out how to effectively reach our target audience.

I researched the kinds of travel agencies celebrities and other very successful people turn to when planning a trip. Those agencies mostly didn't have any Dominican Republic properties included in their listings. I knew if I could show them these properties, they would be interested. I began making cold calls to these agencies to let them know about the luxury homes we had in our portfolio. Thanks to the way we presented them, some of those agencies wanted to add them to their own portfolios for clients to see.

It was also important to gain a better understanding of the type of client we wanted to serve. I started looking at when and where they travel and found many common threads. The people flying from the DR to the Bahamas were the same people flying to Ibiza, St. Barts, Mykonos, and other exclusive destinations. They liked to entertain while on vacation. Many used the same types of products and services. There was a lot they had in common, and all this information helped us promote the properties and experiences more accurately. We were lucky with our timing because this market was wide open and ready for action. We built a whole brand and business around this concept called P&V (Palms & Villas) and it quickly took off.

One of the many things I learned during my business education was the importance of building and deepening relationships with customers. The way we did this at P&V was by expanding beyond just renting a villa to creating a whole concierge approach to a person's stay in the DR. We helped arrange and provide services such as top-notch chefs to cook amazing meals on-site, transportation to curated tours and excursions around the island, massage sessions on-site, and so on. After all, when targeting the luxury property market, the kind of people coming want more than just a villa rental, they want a whole experience.

We worked hard at building relationships with our target customers and the travel agencies they worked with. We also specialized in concierge services for people visiting the DR. These became the keys that unlocked many opportunities. Those travel agencies don't have an office in every desirable destination around the world. They depend on having local providers who have the knowledge and experience to be their on-the-ground partner to make the necessary arrangements. We decided to position ourselves as the go-to local provider in the luxury villa rental market of the DR who could meet the expectations of top-level clients. And it worked!

Once again, confidence through preparation was the key. The travel agencies were impressed with the properties in our portfolio, and even more so by how beautifully we presented them, as well as all the different concierge services we could provide. Some of these clients would get to know us and tell us they wanted to work with us directly on their next trip. We'd pay a referral fee to the original agency through which they met us, but this is how we began working directly with clients of the type I wanted to serve.

GROWTH MINDSET AND LEAPS OF FAITH

When I look back at those first couple years in the Dominican Republic, it took more than one leap of faith to get started. Knocking on the doors of waterfront properties in the DR to connect with owners took a leap of faith, and so did calling up agencies who serve elite travelers to get them to agree to work with our properties.

What leap of faith should you be making right now to accelerate your movement forward toward your vision, your dream life, and your why? Like the quote at beginning of this chapter, if you don't take the leap of faith, you could miss fulfilling your dreams. I can hear some of you out there saying, "But Alvaro, taking a leap of faith is scary!" While I agree that taking a leap of faith *is* a bit scary, it's also what moves you forward. You've no doubt heard the phrase *nothing ventured, nothing gained.* It's true! You've got to take risks to achieve the dream life you've been designing and visualizing in your head.

Where this idea of the leap of faith fits into my approach to life is under the heading of the *growth mindset.* If you want to grow your business and your life into something wonderful, you've got to cultivate a growth mindset. For me, that means constantly asking myself, am I taking enough risks?

What I realized about taking a leap of faith is how it's not about jumping completely blind into the unknown. That would be foolish, right? It's about being confident you can land on your feet because you've put in the time and effort to prepare for making the jump. What I'm talking about here is a calculated risk based on confidence. You've got to believe in yourself to make it happen. Each leap is about taking a risk and trusting you have what you need to make it work because you're prepared. So, I ask you again, is there a leap of faith you should be taking? If so, keep your vision in mind, be confident you can handle it, take a deep breath, and go for it!

Write down 3 leaps of faith you could take to accelerate leveling up. Also write down what's holding you back from doing each one. Is it fear? Is it a lack of confidence? Whatever they are, turn them into positive affirmations as if you've already conquered them. "I have the courage to…" or "I am confident I can…" and so on.

As for me, I soon decided it was time to level up even further. We had great properties and a better understanding of our target clientele, but what I really wanted was to take it to the next level. I didn't want to be just the local partner in the DR for agencies who might send some of their clients our way. There was a fire inside telling me we should be building our *own* thriving network of local partners in jetsetter destinations. We would need to draw on all our energy, passion, and creativity to develop a formula for success. Would we succeed?

7

ENERGY, PASSION, HONESTY, HUMILITY

"Everything is energy and that's all there is to it.
Match the frequency of the reality you want and you
cannot help but get that reality. It can be no other way.
This is not philosophy. This is physics."

~ Albert Einstein ~

I f expanding the business into an international agency
serving the specific market segment of high-net-worth
individuals (HNWIs) was the goal, then I had to get
busy in lining things up. I needed to travel to the types of
exclusive destinations the target audience traveled to so I
could find and network with the best local partners to add
the right properties to our portfolio as well as the concierge
services. This traveling research project also allowed me to
spend more time getting to know the clientele better. They
thought nothing of paying up to $10,000 a night to stay in
the most luxurious villas; properties you don't find listed just
anywhere on the internet.

During conversations with these people, the opportunity to ask them about their upcoming travel plans would naturally come up. If they mentioned thinking about going to places like Mykonos or Ibiza, I would mention having a friend with an incredible villa they could rent. Then I would mention if they needed help arranging travel on a chartered jet, I could handle that as well. With this level of interest, then the concierge team behind the scenes back in the Dominican Republic could begin making all the necessary arrangements. Many times, the clients would invite me to go on the trip with them. Why? Because they liked my positive energy and how enthusiastic I was in bringing value to them. This led to a relationship that went beyond business into friendship and opened up even more opportunities.

I found myself suddenly living the jet-set lifestyle, but without the same level of endless cashflow backing it, which is a tricky situation to be in. As I was developing relationships with these people, I felt I needed to be like one of them, paying for many things along the way. One week I might be in an amazing villa with clients, and the very next week I might be sleeping on a couch or in a car since I needed to keep reinvesting as much incoming money as possible into the business—whatever it takes to make your dream happen. It just meant sometimes cashflow was a problem. I was really sweating bullets one night when I was out with prospective clients and was going to pick up the check for dinner and drinks. My card was declined. I had them try it again, but it was declined again. I tried a different card, and that one was also declined. The clients ended up paying and I made a joke out of it.

Inside my own head, however, I was freaking out. "What am I doing? Am I going about this whole crazy idea all wrong?" I realized I was pretending to be someone I was not, and it did not feel right—I was experiencing imposter syndrome.

Have you ever had a kind of panicky feeling because you're afraid everyone's going to see through you and know you're a fraud, or you don't belong there, or something similar? That's imposter syndrome, and I had it bad as I sat there sweating while each of my credit cards was being declined. It's a horrible feeling most people want to avoid. Sure, rubbing shoulders with jetsetters in amazing destinations around the world was like living in a dream, but it was not one I could sustain. The clients themselves barely even noticed one way or the other, but it felt like a crisis to me.

As I continued exploring and developing this international network, it also became clear to me there was one thing working against the whole idea, which was being a company based in the Dominican Republic. When the jetsetter clients I wanted to work with turn to an agency to make trip arrangements, they don't call up a company in the Dominican Republic. What I really needed to do was establish this international operation as a company based in the United States. Potential clients and local partners would automatically view a US company as more trustworthy.

The potential path forward I could see would be to separate this developing international luxury operation from the original P&V business model. The luxury division would be established in the US as its own company and brand while P&V would continue focusing on villa rentals in the Dominican Republic.

At the end of my traveling research project, which was every bit as successful as I hoped it would be, I made a stop in Madrid where I met up with my grandfather, Eduardo De Santis. He was not my biological maternal grandfather, but he had been with my grandmother for many years and was a powerful influence in my life. He was from Italy, where he was a successful actor back in the 1950s, then a screenwriter, film producer, and businessman.

In 1961 his interest in social issues led to establish the Gold Mercury International think tank dedicated to corporate responsibility and improving international governance. Gold Mercury Awards have been handed out each year to companies, organizations, governments, and leaders known for advancing good governance practices and peaceful cooperation. In the late 1970s he got into branding and joined Landor, which was a brand consulting firm based in San Francisco. He helped take the company global and worked on some incredible branding and re-branding projects, including Santander Bank, Iberia Airlines, Cepsa petroleum company, Iberdrola energy, and savings bank La Caixa. He came up with the word VISA for the credit cards so many people use today. He also came up with the short-hand way of referring to Coca Cola as Coke. Italy's President Giorgio Napolitano even awarded him the highest civilian recognition, the Order of the Italian Star.

We went out to dinner, and I explained how everything was rapidly developing, from adding international properties to the company portfolio to developing the global network of local partners I needed. I also told him my hunch it would be better to build this new international brand as a company based in the United States. As I was hoping, he brought clarity and wisdom to the table. He confirmed I was right on track. Then he took out a pen and wrote something on a napkin. He looked me in the eye and said, "And this is the name of the company." He slid the napkin over to me, and when I looked down at it, there were the words he wrote on it: Super Luxury Group. It was perfect!

Energized by this encounter with my grandfather, it was time to get things moving. I flew to Miami to get the ball rolling. The next few months were a whirlwind of activity. I got engaged to my girlfriend at the time, and through her I met a guy who was very well-connected in the Miami real estate scene. As we talked, things just clicked between the two of us, and he agreed to be my business partner in the US to continue developing the new company and its brand. With those pieces in place, I could get back to traveling around the world building the global network of local providers we needed, and he could manage the day-to-day local operations of the company. Super Luxury Group was on its way, and I am forever grateful to my grandfather for naming it. Sadly, that dinner was the last conversation I ever had with him because he passed away soon afterwards.

In the middle of all this, I also had an epiphany about another piece of the puzzle, and it had everything to do with marketing. Most of the clients we had worked with came to us through their preferred travel agency. What we needed was better exposure to attract more of these clients to us directly. It dawned on me there was an opportunity to tap into OPAs, meaning other people's audiences. I started looking closer at my target client audience of HNWIs and celebrities to see who they followed on social media. Some of the people they followed had huge audiences on social media. They were clearly *influencers*, and I'd seen some of them at social gatherings I attended when I was traveling around the world to different destinations. This is when I realized the next step for me was to bring *influencer marketing* into the SLG business model.

I had been watching influencer marketing through social media platforms like Instagram grow in other industries, but no one was using it effectively in real estate, which seemed like a huge opportunity to me. Influencer marketing has always been around because it's essentially what word-of-mouth marketing is—people influencing others to purchase some product or service. Celebrity endorsements are a form of influencer marketing, but social media influencers are more effective because they have a closer, more intimate connection with their audience than celebrities have with their fans.

The reach of influencers has increased dramatically in recent years thanks to the internet and social media platforms. Back in 2016 the influencer market industry was maybe worth $1.7 billion. Today that figure is more like $10–$14 billion, with most experts agreeing it will keep growing in the coming years. What accounts for this explosive growth of influencer marketing? The answer is simple: It works! It's at least as effective if not more effective than other forms of marketing. On average, businesses see an ROI (return on investment) of $5.78 for every dollar spent on influencer marketing.

The idea taking shape in my mind was to make better use of luxury villas when they were vacant. These kinds of properties are often only rented out maybe 40% of the time, so there was plenty of availability. I thought to myself, "Why not let an influencer spend a week or two at a property if it was just going to sit empty anyway? And what influencer wouldn't want to stay in an exclusive villa for free if they could?" The influencer would just live their life and do what they do, but they'd be doing it in one of our specially branded villas. This would naturally result in some amazing exposure for our properties and our business brand. When I spoke with influencers about this idea, they were all-in because it was too good to resist.

To my surprise, however, when I started pitching this idea to some of the property owners as a big marketing opportunity, almost all of them immediately said no. They didn't understand what influencers were or why it might work. They couldn't get their brains around letting someone stay in their villa for free, even though I explained it would only happen during down times in the schedule. Luckily, there were a few who could see the opportunity as clearly as I did, and they agreed to try it. Those early cases quickly proved the point. After influencers stayed at a property, the occupancy rate for that villa would skyrocket—and even more so when we brought luxury brand tie-ins into the mix (luxury cars, clothing, yachts, and so on). It was an extremely effective way to leverage the luxury lifestyle angle into attracting our target audience and growing our customer base.

Now I felt like I really had the solid model I needed. It consisted of four pillars: Luxury properties, luxury brands, influencers, and high-net-worth individuals. Yes!

MAIN VALUES AND MY WHY

Passion and energy both took on new meaning and became more important than ever to me while I was traveling around the world. What I realized was this: Positive energy is the current currency for professional and personal success. Positive energy, enthusiasm, and being upbeat opened many doors of opportunity for me during this time.

Passion is woven throughout important aspects of my approach to self-development. It's a core part of my *Why*. When I explain why I do what I do, it goes something like this: I started a luxury hospitality company because I love to travel, connect with people, and have unforgettable, life-changing experiences. I want to provide the same opportunities to those who share a passion for traveling and discovering what life has to offer.

I list passion as one of my *main values*, and it's also a strong piece of my *growth mindset*:

To create a business that fuels your passion!

The quote from Albert Einstein at the beginning of this chapter is about the importance of energy being the gateway to achievement. Oprah Winfrey adds to this idea when she says, "Passion is energy. Feel the power that comes from focusing on what excites you." Passion and energy is a powerful combination.

What are you passionate about in life? This is one of the most important questions anyone can ask and answer for themselves. How do you find your passion? Just be aware of what gives you energy when you're doing it. Like Oprah said, passion is energy. Find those things that make you feel alive and fulfilled and energized. Those are the things that will fuel your progress toward your vision.

But I also learned some hard lessons during my travels. Energy and passion were opening all kinds of doors, but I was also getting myself into difficult places with cashflow, which was very stressful. When I stopped and took some time to reflect on what was going on, I realized several things. One was a false assumption about how to interact with the jetsetters I was meeting during my travels. I was approaching it from a "pay-to-play" mentality. If I was going to work with this type of client and also live this kind of lifestyle, I assumed I needed to basically be one of them, or at least *appear* to be one of them. That's why I was trying to pay for way more than I should have. I was not being true to my authentic self.

What happened was I had allowed my life to get out of balance once again. I was following the energy and passion, and yet I wasn't being my true self either. This is when I reminded myself of another one of my main values, *honesty*. I wasn't being honest with myself or the people I was meeting and spending time with when I tried to be someone I wasn't. What I needed was to be honest about my limitations and humbly accept help when offered. It was wrong of me to try to impress jetsetters by spending like them. I couldn't do it and trying to do it was landing me in some very embarrassing situations. Why not go out on a limb, stop trying to play the part, and just be open and honest about what I could and couldn't do?

Realizing what I needed to do was a huge relief because I immediately felt more aligned with my values. Doing it, however, was not so easy. I had to set aside my pride and just be completely up-front about my situation. As it turned out, all my anxiety about it was of my own making. These people still loved my energy and passion and were always happy to just pay for things when I was up-front about it. In fact, they appreciated me being honest and humble about it. The more I thought about it, the more I understood how unrealistic it was for me to act like I had it all figured out when I was only twenty-five years old at the time!

Take a moment to **review your vision, your why, and your main values**. Keeping these elements front-and-center as often as possible is the key to leveling up to your dream life.

* * * * *

Now the momentum was really building up. Everything was moving fast, and it was exciting. I was engaged, I had the company up and running in the US, the business model was solid, we were even featured in *Forbes* and other publications alongside other well-known and up-and-coming companies. More importantly, we were also getting lots of reservations from jetsetters making their travel plans for the next year. I was flying all over the world meeting clients and local partners, but now I was doing it right. I kept my main values front and center while using social currency rather than living beyond my means. But as often happens, just when everything seemed to be moving along in all the right directions, something came along to derail everything, and it was a microscopic organism called the novel coronavirus. And that was just *one* of several obstacles that 2020 held in store for me—so fasten your seatbelts for a wild ride!

8

RIDING THE ROLLERCOASTER

"Life is like a roller coaster. It's never going to be perfect—
it is going to have perfect moments, and then rough spots,
but it's all worth it."

~ Patti Smith ~

E very time a new year begins is an exciting time of
anticipating all the incredible things you're going to
accomplish and experience. For me, everything was
falling into place with the Super Luxury Group business model
and ramping up operations with rapid growth in new clients
and reservations. Now it was time for me to start tackling the
challenge of returning to the United States, but this time for
good. But how would I get back in on a more permanent basis
after having been forced out only a couple years earlier? It
comes down to money and logistics. The clearest path forward
for me would be to obtain an investor visa since the reason I
wanted to come back was to run my growing business.

The strange thing about the investor visa is how the
hoops you need to jump through require all sorts of things

to already be in place in the US. This felt counter-intuitive if I wasn't allowed to legally be in the country to begin with. There had to be an established office location with a long-term lease, real expenses, an established US bank account, 5–10 US employees, a five-year business plan showing how much money I'd be investing in the business, projected growth of the company, a realistic view of the risks involved, and the positive impact this business will have on the US economy— but most important was the money. I needed to make a large investment of my own assets into the business. Putting all the pieces of this kind of puzzle in place takes time. I had a good head start on many of these items, now I needed to start putting most of my own assets into the business to prove I was serious about it.

Right when I was beginning to feel confident about having these pieces in place so I could apply for the investor visa, the COVID-19 global pandemic hit! Everything related to visas and travel completely shut down. Embassies were closed and not taking appointments. Even getting back into the US just to manage some of the details related to the business was impossible. I was stuck in the Dominican Republic and unable to take the next steps.

With air travel all but shut down, the impact on the business was immediate and painful. Within a matter of weeks, all the upcoming reservations were cancelled by customers. Even worse, we had to refund the deposits made on every one of those reservations. It's demoralizing to see the inflow of money to your business come to a screeching halt. It's downright nerve racking to watch what money your business has left flowing right back out of the company in the form of refunds to customers. The situation was looking bleak.

This became a time of reflection for me. I had to ask myself, "Am I still on the right path? How can I possibly make this work?" And then when I looked around me, I had to admit it was a beautiful life I could have right there in the Dominican Republic. I lived in Cap Cana, the most luxurious residential area on the island. In fact, it was one of the best areas in all the Caribbean. You can literally live like a king there for a fraction of what it would cost to live a similar lifestyle in places like New York City or even Miami. I looked around Cap Cana and saw many other people who had settled there and were living wonderful lives. I could easily do the same.

But you see, the operative word here is "settled." If I stayed in the DR, then I would be settling for something less than my vision. Would it be a lovely life? Yes! Would I be very comfortable? Yes! But was it the fulfillment of my vision? No. I didn't want to settle for just being comfortable, tempting as it was. I didn't want to wake up ten years later and find myself doing the same thing and realizing I hadn't fulfilled my dreams. So, I reminded myself how "comfort" is kryptonite. I wouldn't be able to level up to my vision if I stayed in the Dominican Republic.

During the worst of the pandemic, I had more time than usual to spend working on my own personal development. Deep down inside I knew if I was going to succeed in moving everything forward toward my vision, I needed to become the very best version of myself as possible. This is when I read and listened to many insightful self-development books and explored all kinds of resources and tools. It was during this time I discovered the importance of staying true to core values, and how developing powerful habits and routines could all be harnessed to not only stay on track but accelerate leveling up.

Despite this intensive self-development process, it still wasn't clear to me whether this investor visa path back into the US was going to work. At this stage I went ahead and took all my money and invested it into the business so I could proceed with the application. I needed to maintain the office in the US with employees and expenses (even though everything was shut down thanks to COVID). I couldn't even get into the country as tourist. I called my immigration lawyer and told her, "Alexandra, I want to keep moving forward with the investor visa as quickly as possible. I don't care what's happening in the world, we're going to make it happen!" She didn't sound very confident in my decision. I looked at my bank account and it was down to just over a thousand dollars. It was all I had left after putting all my other assets into SLG.

Leaning into my vision in these conditions required an enormous amount of trust it would somehow all work out. It meant staying focused on the bigger picture. It meant tolerating discomfort and challenges instead of settling for something comfortable. Of course, people thought I was crazy to try building Super Luxury Group (SLG) with a global pandemic raging. I couldn't allow myself to listen to them or be influenced by them. Every time I talked to my business partner in Miami, I could sense he was somewhat frustrated with me not being there to help, but we also began noticing something that made us reconsider the primary focus of SLG.

What we were seeing was the rapid rise of Miami as a destination itself. The jetsetters couldn't travel as freely as they normally did all over the world, but Miami was becoming increasingly popular. It was more open than most places, which made it a more viable option. I started to see a path forward in which SLG could be primarily about Miami luxury real estate as opposed to international villa rentals. Taking the same marketing tactics that I had developed for villa rentals and applying them to the best properties in Miami suddenly looked like a smart business move. My business partner naturally liked the idea as well, especially with his decade's worth of experience and contacts in the Miami real estate market. Finally, a path forward!

Then I got a call from my best friend during graduate school who informed me Miguel, who had been his roommate and our good friend at Lynn University, had passed away. At first, I thought he meant passed out, like from drinking too much or something. Unfortunately, he meant passed away as in he had died. He had been killed in a motorcycle accident. The three of us had been very close friends throughout our time at Lynn. This news was devastating. I had literally spoken with him the day before. We had talked about how good it would be to see him once I got this investor visa and could come back to the US for good. Now he was gone forever, just like so many others had lost friends and family during 2020.

Once I recovered from the initial shock, the reality of the situation quickly sunk in. Miguel had come to the US from Zimbabwe on a scholarship to attend Lynn University. His father had passed away some years before, and his mother was struggling to keep the household going financially. She didn't have the resources to come to the United States to claim her son's body or have a funeral. A bunch of us who had been friends at Lynn got together online over Zoom to figure out what we could do to help Miguel's family. Flying a body to Zimbabwe is quite expensive, so we set up an online campaign raise support. And I knew what I had to do.

You see, in this moment I was reminded of a simple truth: There are more important things in life than your bank account balance. So, I donated my last $1,000 to the campaign. I have a screenshot from June 28, 2020, showing what I had left after making the donation: fourteen dollars and seventy-three cents. Everything else had been invested into SLG. But it felt right to honor my friend's life by helping return his body to his family in Zimbabwe. I saved that screenshot and still have it because it reminds me to keep things in perspective. It is a visual reminder that any life can be cut short in the blink of an eye. It reminds me to live life to the fullest in the present moment because *now* is the only thing we really have.

Toward the end of the summer in 2020 when travel restrictions began to ease, I went back to Spain because as my native country that's where I needed to be for the next steps of the investor visa process. My fiancée flew to Europe from the US so we could finally spend some time together. We were both excited about me moving forward on the visa so I could get back into the US and we could start making a new life together. The next step in the process was the interview.

My appointment was for the beginning of September, but with the fall came a new COVID surge and new restrictions. My appointment was cancelled and rescheduled for a month later, at the beginning of October. Then *that* appointment was also postponed, this time to mid-October. At that point, my fiancée had to go back to the US, and I ended up couch-surfing from one relative's place to another. At least I got to spend some wonderful time with my siblings, but I didn't want to overstay my welcome. Even my mid-October appointment was cancelled and rescheduled, this time to November 3, which was election day in the US.

When the day finally came, the interview went well, and I got the investor visa on the spot! What a huge relief. I called my fiancée to tell her the good news, but I didn't hear back from her immediately, which was unusual, but I didn't give it another thought in the moment. Meanwhile, I got in touch with all the other important people in my life about the good news and a couple days later I was on a flight to Miami—and this time it would be for good!

I could barely contain my excitement as the plane landed in Miami. I was already in touch with the owner of a great place my fiancée and I were going to move into, and we could get back into planning our wedding. I'd finally be able to work directly with my business partner on the ground, not to mention the whole team at SLG who had never even met me in person yet—all good stuff to take my life and business to the next level.

I went to where my fiancée lived and where I also was keeping a lot my personal stuff, but she wasn't there. I kept calling her, but she wasn't picking up. I went to check in with her family, who were all so happy to see me since I had a great relationship with all of them. They invited me to have dinner with the whole family, which would be a great way to surprise my fiancée.

One of my fiancée sisters took me aside and said, "Look, I don't know what your situation is with my sister or if the two of you have talked, and I don't want to be the one telling you this, but I think it would be better for you to leave before she arrives."

This was not something I was expecting. "I just don't understand any of this. What's going on? What's happening?" I felt bad for her because she was extremely uncomfortable with this conversation, but I had to find out what was up.

With a sad, guilty look she said, "Alvaro, I think you and I both know what's going on, and I'm very sorry for you."

I was so taken aback with those words, all I could say was, "What?" Then it hit me. The lack of contact from my fiancée could only mean one thing. "She's with someone else isn't she."

The sister nodded her head in agreement and replied, "But don't take my word for it. She must know you're back now, so just give her a little time and I'm sure she'll contact you."

I was in shock and had to get out of there. I gathered all my stuff, packed it into my car, and took off to go to a place my aunt and uncle had in Key Biscayne. It felt like the longest drive of my life. I was destroyed. I finally made it back to the US for good, and the one person I most want to see, the woman to whom I am engaged, not only isn't there to greet me but is with someone else? And she doesn't even have the courage to tell me what's going on? These thoughts just kept spinning through my mind. I was riding a wild emotional roller coaster and I couldn't get off. I was cycling through all the negative emotions: shock, anger, sadness, despair. You name it, I felt it over and over on that drive to Key Biscayne.

After completing the drive and getting settled in, I asked myself, "What should I do?" I was still feeling a lot of pain, but I also knew it was up to me to *choose* how I would respond to this unexpected development. Was I going to let this break me or build me? Was I going to let it be a setback or a springboard?

I chose to take all the negative emotional energy I felt and channel it into a big constructive challenge of some kind. I Googled "toughest challenge in the world" and what came up in the results was the Ironman triathlon, a grueling physical challenge consisting of a 2.4-mile swim followed by a 112-mile bicycle ride followed by a 26.22-mile run—and you've got to do it in less than seventeen hours. It's basically the most difficult one-day sporting event in the world. I signed up for one right there on the spot, never mind I had zero experience with swimming or biking and barely had any distance running experience.

Meanwhile, my business partner decided he no longer wanted to be involved in Super Luxury Group. He had recently become a father and his priorities shifted to maximizing his income rather than helping build the brand and business model of SLG. The real estate market in Miami had suddenly become red hot, and he saw dollar signs everywhere. The problem was the transactions he was racking up should have been considered part of SLG's operations, but he claimed they were all customers he had worked with in his other business before he joined SLG. It was not a legitimate argument at all, and I had to decide how to handle yet another painful situation.

I made it clear I disapproved of what he was doing and how disappointed I was at him for trying to take advantage of the business for his own gain. SLG would take a huge financial hit if he took a bunch of our big clients with him, but it was better for me to now take full control of the business. Why? Because having that negative energy around wouldn't be helpful to me or the business. It was better for us to just part ways so I could focus all my attention and energy on building the SLG brand without any distractions.

2020: A ROLLER COASTER YEAR

Most everyone goes through a time in their life where it feels like everything goes wrong all at the same time. I think a whole lot of people experienced 2020 as a year-long train wreck of epic proportions. There were times when I certainly felt that way about 2020. Along comes COVID and our business came to a screeching halt and lost nearly all its money. One of my best friends from graduate school had his life snuffed out in the prime of his life, not to mention so many other people dying during the pandemic. My parents got divorced. My fiancée cheated on me and then left me for another man. And my business partner abruptly quit and took all his clients with him. Sounds like a terrible, horrible, no good, very bad year, right?

Despite all the bad and frustrating things that happened during 2020, there were some good things in there too, like getting the investor visa to permanently return to the US. Even more important was how the SLG business model was able to pivot so quickly from international luxury villa rentals to Miami luxury real estate sales. In hindsight it was a huge win, but it was hard to see it that way at the time because of all the other crazy stuff that was happening.

Losing both my fiancée and my business partner felt like serious blows. The pandemic was awful. You have zero control over when life throws obstacles at you. What you *do* have control over is choosing how you respond. What you do next after a crisis is incredibly important. Will you let it break you down or build you up? Will you let it be an obstacle or turn it into a superpower? It is in these moments when you have an opportunity to level up and be the very best version of yourself. The choice I try to make in these situations is to embrace the pain, and you'll discover why in the next chapter.

9

EMBRACING THE PAIN TO REACH NEW HEIGHTS

"Pain is often the precursor to personal growth.
Don't dread it. Instead, embrace it."

~ Robin S. Sharma ~

I don't know about you, but for me, turning the calendar to 2021 was a liberating experience. Putting 2020 firmly behind me was a huge relief. I do agree with Robin Sharma that pain can be a precursor to personal growth, but I would extend it to every area on the Wheel of Life, including the career, social, family, intellectual, physical, spiritual, and financial aspects of life. There was more pain in 2020 than I or anyone else could have ever anticipated. Now it was time to do something with it. I was determined to be like Japanese novelist Kenji Miyazawa who said, "We must embrace pain and burn it as fuel for our journey." If I could use all the pain from 2020 as fuel, then I ought to reach all kinds of new heights—and I am grateful that it happened.

What I realized was this: *The quality of your life will be dependent on the choices you make in the painful moments.* When you go through a difficult period in life, I have found the best path forward is to hit the ground running with even bigger dreams and goals than I had before. It can feel counterintuitive at first, but if you're going to get the most mileage out of using pain as fuel, dreaming big and setting up massive goals is how you turn those obstacles into super-powers. I embraced my wildest dreams, and I didn't want to waste a single moment. After all, one of the most important lessons so many of us learned during 2020 is how life is too short to put your dreams on hold.

You cannot know what tomorrow will bring, whether good or bad, but what you can always do is move forward in the present moment. The only thing you ever really have is *now*. Let that realization sink in. Let it make you dream even bigger than before. Let it make you *hungry* to set and achieve massive goals. Combine your pain and your passion into high-octane fuel to turbocharge forward momentum toward your vision. Don't wait for some future moment that may never come. Do it *now*. For me, here are some of the goals I set as I emerged from all the pain and difficulties of 2020:

- Sell a "double-digit" home, meaning a home worth at least $10 million.
- Speak at a conference in front of thousands people.
- Travel to a dozen luxury destinations and attend at least two red-carpet events.
- Meet ten people from my relationship vision list.
- Achieve one million followers and get verified on all social media accounts.
- Read or listen to 100 books.
- Complete 200 skydive jumps, including from a heli-copter and a hot air balloon.

- Complete an Ironman triathlon.
- Be featured in ten top magazines and appear on the cover of one.
- Support both my parents financially.
- Climb one of the "Seven Summits" (highest mountain on each continent).
- Obtain my helicopter pilot license.
- Write a book.

It might look a bit ambitious, right? But here's the thing: If you don't set challenging goals that make you stretch beyond your comfort zone, you'll never experience the fire that comes when you achieve them. Remember, comfort is kryptonite that robs you of your superpowers.

Some of the goals listed above are personal, some are directly related to my business, and some are a combination of both. They also all relate to one or more areas on the Wheel of Life. I chose skydiving from a helicopter as the goal I wanted to use as a way of saying goodbye to 2020 and welcome to 2021. Why skydiving? There are several reasons. One is because it is by far one of the most thrilling things I have ever experienced. The rush of adrenaline makes me feel more alive than anything else I can think of. It gives me a different perspective on the world as I free-fall through the air toward the surface of this incredible planet we call home.

Skydiving makes me see the possibilities. It makes me want to say *yes* to life, to achieving my dreams, to making an impact on and a difference in this world. You will never be as fully aware of life and its possibilities as you are when skydiving. It lights my brain on fire and fuels whatever I do next with more passion, energy, and excitement than anything else I might do. For me, skydiving is one way I live a fuel-injected, turbocharged life.

So, on December 31, 2020, the last day of a year no one will ever forget, I jumped out of a helicopter and parachuted to the ground. I had obtained my skydiving license back in 2017 and had previously done all my skydiving from airplanes, so this was a way of bringing a new and unique twist to one of my favorite ways of feeling fully alive. When I landed, I was ready to make my wildest dreams come true. Here's a video clip of this jump:

What I wasn't expecting so early in 2021 was getting into another relationship. After the break-up with my former fiancée, I not only signed up for my first Ironman triathlon, but I also promised myself I would remain open to whatever life might bring me. I wasn't going to let the pain of a past experience, no matter how recent it was, hold me back from whatever might happen.

As fate would have it, there was a very successful influencer who had just been named Forbes Lifestyle Influencer of the Year, Hofit Golan, who our team had been in touch with recently because we wanted to collaborate with her on SLG projects. She was in Miami during the final days of 2020, and we agreed to meet. Right away things just "clicked" between us. We ended up celebrating the arrival of the New Year together and got to talking about what our wildest dreams were for 2021. I couldn't resist asking if she wanted to try skydiving. She wasn't sure at first, but then as I told her what it would be like she said, "Why not? I'm here, so let's do it!" So, our first date on January 1, 2021, was an incredible tandem jump out of a plane. Ever since then we've both been living life to the fullest.

Part of why we make such a good pair is because we're both completely comfortable and happy with who we are as individuals. This is so much more important than I ever realized before. Neither of us "needs" the other. We are both complete without one another, and yet happier together. Neither of us has an agenda or makes demands on the other. It's a very refreshing relationship experience.

Skydiving has continued to play an important role in both my personal and professional life. I celebrated the arrival of 2022 with another unique skydiving experience, this time from a hot air balloon. I made quite a show of it, and the video of this one went viral on social media. Below is a post about it on my Instagram page:

Climbing my first "Seven Summits" peak was another huge accomplishment for me. Mount Kilimanjaro in Tanzania is ranked as the fourth most prominent mountain in the world with an elevation of 19,341 feet (5,895 meters) and is the tallest mountain on the continent of Africa. When you decide to tackle this kind of challenge, you want to do it with someone who not only knows what they're doing in a technical sense, but someone who brings a fresh perspective to everything they do. For me, that person turned out to be Sean Swarner.

Sean is one of the most incredible people you could ever hope to meet. When he was only thirteen years old, he was diagnosed with a stage-four terminal case of cancer in the form of Hodgkin's disease (a cancer of the immune system). He was expected to live no more than a few months, but he somehow made a miraculous recovery. Then at age sixteen he again found himself battling a deadly cancer, this time in the form of Askin's sarcoma. For him it was a golf-ball-sized cancerous tumor on his right lung. They removed the tumor, leaving him with only one functional lung, and expected him to live for less than two weeks. A priest even came and told him his last rites. And yet somehow Sean managed to not only survive but thrive.

Recognized as one of the most inspirational people in the world, what Sean realized was that beating cancer not once but twice meant no challenge would ever be too great for him, no peak too high to climb. A decade later he became the first cancer survivor to climb Mount Everest, and he did it with only one lung. He has since gone on to climb all the highest peaks in Africa, Europe, South America, Australia, Antarctica, and North America to complete the Seven Summits challenge. He went on to ski to both the South and the North Poles, which meant he had then also completed the Explorer's Grand Slam. Needless to say, I was in good company for my first Seven Summits peak—the first of many adventures to come for both of us.

Climbing Kilimanjaro with Sean was a truly amazing experience. Connecting deeply with nature is always a rejuvenating experience for me, and the views of gorgeous landscapes as we hiked were incredible. What did I learn from this experience? One thing that comes to mind is patience. This was interesting for me because I'm not a patient guy when it comes to doing whatever it takes to reach my goals, dreams, and vision. But Kilimanjaro taught me patience. It took a full five days of hiking and climbing to reach the summit. There were many times along the way where it felt like nothing was changing and the peak we had set our sights on still looked impossibly far away. This is when I came to an important realization: *You don't conquer the mountain, you conquer yourself.* In this case, I needed to be patient, which can sometimes be difficult. I had to remind myself that every step we took was in fact getting us closer to our ultimate destination, even though it didn't seem that way much of the time.

This point about patience is important because when you're going about setting and achieving goals, and when you're dreaming big and have a vision for your life, it can often feel the way I felt in Tanzania—plodding along toward the peak of Kilimanjaro but feeling like we weren't making any progress, even though I knew we were. People say patience is a virtue, and I never truly understood what it meant until hiking up Kilimanjaro. Below you can see the Instagram story summarizing my whole trip to Tanzania, which also included going on safari in the Serengeti:

One of my goals was to have a stronger presence as a speaker at significant conferences and events. I remember several years ago when I first met Grant Cardone, I was thoroughly impressed with his energy, his knowledge, his accomplishments, and his ability to inspire. He owns and operates seven different privately held companies that collectively achieve more than $100 million in sales every year. He also has a $5.1 billion portfolio of multifamily properties. The fact he got his start as an entrepreneur in real estate made me like him even more.

When I saw Grant speak at a real estate conference here in Miami, I said to myself, "In a few years I'll be speaking with him on stage." And in 2022, it happened! I shared the exact same stage with him and two other panelists to speak about the evolution of real estate in recent years, and more than 5,000 people were watching the event. This is the kind of thing that can happen by using the power of manifestation by visualizing and affirming what you want to happen. When you do this, everything happens twice—first in your mind, and then in reality.

I do recommend seeing Grant speak if you ever have the opportunity, or at least reading his books. Since sharing the stage with him, I've been speaking at more conferences with incredible people, such as Tony Giordano. He's another remarkable person who got his start in real estate who has helped agents and partner associates sell $1.3 billion in properties since 2010. Now he owns a whole range of different businesses, is a sough-after consultant and speaker, and a best-selling author.

Another item I wanted to focus on more in 2021 was really living the luxury lifestyle because it's an important way of building my personal brand and attracting the kind of people I wanted to be working with as clients in SLG. Working with so many different influencers on luxury lifestyle content for the business, I saw first-hand how they build their personal brand and leverage that into new opportunities. And since Hofit is herself an influencer, she is doing the same as well, so this is another way in which she and I are perfectly aligned in our relationship. We travel the globe together to experience the pinnacle of luxury in each location we explore, staying at the best hotels and resorts in jetsetter destinations such as Dubai, Bali, Greece, Maldives, Turkey, France, Italy, and elsewhere.

We also get to attend some of the most exclusive red-carpet events in the world, such as the Cannes Film Festival in France and the Venice Film Festival in Italy, where I was also named the I-Success Entrepreneur of the Year. It was at these events where I got to meet people from my relationship vision list and build significant relationships with them.

Each of these trips is made up of all kinds of luxury experiences, and we use our social currency to pay for most of it. In other words, we work out collaborative ventures with properties that want to host influencers to generate luxury lifestyle content for marketing purposes, just as I had previously been arranging when the SLG business model was international luxury villa rentals. On my Instagram page, there's a Story posted for each destination to give you a summary glimpse of what I see, do, and experience on these wonderful adventures. Visualizing the lifestyle and then living it is what leads to further networking and relationship building that opens doors to new experiences, new clients, and even bigger dreams.

Living the luxury lifestyle also opened doors for me and SLG to be featured in various magazines and other media outlets, including Entrepreneur, Travel & Leisure, Forbes, Thrive Global, IBT, The Daily Mail, and many others. I also pulled a little stunt where I did a skydiving jump hanging onto the side of an airplane and dressed in a business suit that paid big dividends. It ended up reaching more than 250 million views across multiple social media platforms, which is what helped me increase my following and, with the previous media coverage, achieve verification on all my social media accounts. In fact, *Forbes* picked up on it and worked up a whole feature story and named me The Action Man of Luxury Real Estate—a very humbling and gratifying experience. Check it out below:

It's that kind of exposure that led to me selling my first double-digit home. A European acquaintance of mine was in Miami and expressed interest in buying a Miami home, so I took him house shopping. We connected on a lot of different levels and had many shared interests. He did fall in love with one of the properties but wasn't ready to close the deal at that time and returned to Europe. Then he called me out of the blue one day to discuss the deal, and I was literally about to jump out of a plane. I told him I was skydiving and would call him back when I landed. I did, and we closed the deal on a $22 million home. Keep in mind, most people take twenty years to work their way up to selling a double-digit home, and I did it in my first year in real estate! I give some of the credit to the incredible positive energy I had from skydiving for closing that deal. Even better, making that sale allowed me to fulfill my goal of supporting my parents financially.

As you might recall I had previously made a commitment to complete my first Ironman triathlon—considered the toughest one-day sporting event in the world (2.4-mile swim, 112-mile bicycle ride, and a 26-mile run), which must be completed in under 17 hours. I signed up for the Mallorca Ironman in Spain, taking place on October 16. Keep in mind, when I signed up for this, I had never run a distance longer than six miles, and certainly had never done any kind of distance swimming or bicycling.

I called up a friend of mine who I remembered had once told me years ago he was going to do an Ironman. But when I spoke to him, I learned he never ended up doing one. He had worked with coaches and trained for it but just kept encountering different challenges along the way, and he let those challenges derail him from achieving his goal. At the time, I was also reading Arnold Schwarzenegger's memoir, *Total Recall*, and in it he mentioned several times how it's often better to *not* find out about all the difficulties and challenges you might encounter when you decide to do something big like an Ironman triathlon. Why? They can literally psych you out and prevent you from following through. I didn't want that to happen to me.

So, the day after I signed up for the Ironman, I just put on my running shoes and decided to run as far as I could. I told myself if I got tired, I would just keep running. I said if I run so far that I feel like I'm going to throw up, then I would throw up and just keep running. My goal was to run until I couldn't go on, and without knowing how far I went. When I finally had to stop, it turned out I had run a half-marathon (13 miles). Granted, I couldn't walk the next day, but *I did it*. This showed me my body could adjust and perform whatever I needed it to do if I had the willpower to just keep going. How? For me, I would recall the painful events that pushed me to sign up for an Ironman in the first place, then I burned that pain as fuel to keep going.

A half-marathon is now like a warm-up run to me. I got into the habit of running a half-marathon every Monday, and to make the most effective use of my time I would listen to audio books as I ran, which is what allowed me to hit my 100 books goal. Since then, however, I have upgraded to a full marathon every Monday, and I encourage anyone to join me on a #MarathonMonday. It also taught me that when you set a massive goal like this, you've got to just dive in and go after it with everything you've got. If you don't then the challenges encountered along the way can all too easily become excuses for not achieving the goal. For me, I knew if I could run a half-marathon with no previous training, then even a little training would go a long way. It makes you mentally stronger to know you can push through to a huge goal.

Yes, I trained for the Mallorca Ironman, but not to the exclusion of everything else in my life. I wanted to keep my Wheel of Life in balance across all areas. For me, this meant being smart about putting constraints on what I did and didn't do. For some, traveling around the world living the luxury lifestyle means indulging in all kinds of less-than-healthy practices, including heavy meals, drinking, and late-night partying. Probably the most important thing I did to prepare for the Ironman was to *not* indulge in all of that. You can't expect peak physical performance from your body without treating it right, which means optimal nutrition and hydration, regular workouts, plenty of sleep, and so on.

During the summer, I was talking to one of my brothers in Spain who was going to do the Madrid Half (half-ironman distance), but it was rescheduled for later due to the pandemic. As it turned out, the new date was September 25th and there were a few spots available since some people had to cancel because the date-shift didn't work for them, and I went ahead and signed up. I figured doing a half-ironman triathlon distance would be good preparation for the full Ironman three weeks later. It seemed like a good idea, but when I crossed the finish line of the race, I was destroyed. I was a wreck! I felt ill and shaky and thought to myself, "How in the world am I going to do double the distance if I feel this horrible after a half-ironman?" But I shut that line of thinking down immediately and told myself I was going to do it, no matter what.

When I arrived in Mallorca for the full Ironman, there had been shipping issues and I couldn't bring my bike. I had to go find and rent a bike the day before the event—a bike I was going to spend 112 miles (180km) on the next day! But it didn't matter. Why? Because I had already visualized myself crossing the finish line of the Mallorca Ironman. And because I had visualized it over and over again in my mind, I knew it would happen. This visualization process is a critical key to achieving any massive goal. Everything happens twice—first in your mind, then in reality.

And trust me when I say, I needed to keep visualizing myself crossing the finish line throughout the entire event, because some crazy things happened. First off, the event begins with the swim (2.4 miles/3.9km). I decided I was going to start behind the strongest swimmers at the front, thinking I might benefit from swimming in their wake, like drafting off an eighteen-wheeler semi-truck when driving on the highway. What I didn't know is that all the people swimming behind me wanted to get to the front. Dozens of people just swam right overtop me, I was getting kicked all over my body. These people were like savages! They knocked my glasses off, so I had to grope around and find them, or I'd really be screwed. I got kicked in the face multiple times and my nose was bleeding, I got pushed under water repeatedly—it was *brutal*, and this was literally just the first fifteen minutes! How in the world was I going to get through the whole thing if I couldn't even survive the start of the first part?

Lucky for me, I had solidified my mental image of crossing the finish line even before the race began. I went to where the finish line was set up, and I walked across it. I had the mental picture in my mind of what the actual finish line would look like as I approached it. After recovering from the shock of those brutal opening minutes of the swim, I focused on that image of the finish line and just kept telling myself, "I am going to finish this." With that perspective, I found myself there in the water, swimming along and laughing about what just happened. I could laugh at it because I *knew* I was going to finish the race. And this was even though before this day, the longest I had ever swum was what I did two weeks earlier in the Madrid Half Triathlon.

I found myself chanting a kind of mantra along the way, which was *whatever it takes*. I finished the swim and started the bike ride (112 miles/180km). Everything was great until we started some big uphill climbs into the mountains. During one stretch, there was a whole herd of goats blocking the road as they crossed it. Bikers were trying to go around them or through them without slowing down. Quite a few riders wiped out trying to avoid the goats, others crashed into the goats, unable to stop in time. One rider ended up going off the road and over the side of the mountain. It was utter chaos!

After the goat incident, we crested the mountain and got to enjoy a nice big downhill ride. It would have been great, except for a bee that got under my helmet and stung me in the head. Good thing I'm not allergic! It was painful but not debilitating. At the end of the biking portion of the event, I wasted no time in changing into my running shoes and starting the final leg of the event—running a full marathon of 26 miles (42 kilometers).

I was used to running half-marathons on a weekly basis, but when I hit the half-way point, something unexpected happened. My right leg began to cramp, and then my left leg started to cramp. I realized I probably hadn't been hydrating enough or giving myself enough nutrients along the way. At the next aid station, I loaded up on both food and drinks, but I overdid it. My body couldn't absorb it all fast enough, so a good deal of it wanted to run right through me, which meant I needed to find a bathroom, and fast!

This involved looking for one of those plastic porta-potties like you see at construction sites or big outdoor events. As you can imagine, they are poorly maintained and had already been used by hundreds of athletes all in a rush to keep going, which means they were beyond disgusting. I didn't have a choice, though, because I was on the verge of exploding. I finally got inside one, but then getting my tight-fitting athletic tri-suit undone and down so I could use the toilet became a huge undertaking. In the process I ended up having what I can only describe as a full body cramp, and I fell inside this hellhole. Yes, I was now on the floor in all the waste from other people. I was covered in piss and shit and feeling incredibly humiliated. For a moment, the whole thing felt hopeless.

But then I saw that mental image of me crossing the finish line. My mantra of *whatever it takes* came back into my mind. I told myself, I am going to finish this race, but not like this. I pulled myself together, got out of the hellhole, grabbed three bottles of water and poured them all over me to wash off the worst of what was on me. Then I started running again, carefully pacing myself and rationing just the right amount of food and water along the way to keep me going without overtaxing my system. I was still a mess, but I kept going. There were times when I didn't really feel well, and a couple times when everything started to go dark like I was going to lose consciousness. But incredibly, after 12 brutal hours I did it! I crossed that finish line with crowds cheering and a voice booming over the loudspeakers announcing, "Alvaro Nunez, you are an Ironman!" Wow! The level of emotion you feel is overwhelming in that moment. I cried. The whole thing was insane, but I did it.

Then I went on to do another Ironman in Puerto Rico during March 2022 and an Ironman in Panama City Beach, Florida in November 2022 (this last one finishing it in just under *eleven* hours), which means I ended up completing three Ironman races in the space of one year!

It was during the final miles of the Mallorca Ironman that I unlocked my true self, and it was related to the mantra that helped me get through it. It was the whatever-it-takes mindset. This Ironman taught me I could do anything I set my mind to because of the willingness to do whatever it takes to reach those goals, dreams, and vision. What about you? Are you willing to do whatever it takes to achieve your dream lifestyle? Are you feeling a *fire* burning inside to make your dreams come true? Good! Keep on reading because the next and final part of this book is where things get real. I'll share with you the techniques, practices, habits, routines, and hacks that have helped me to not only enjoy all the experiences and achievements mentioned in this chapter, but to dream even bigger and set even more massive goals.

Oh, and did I mention I also got my helicopter license? Trust me, that was one hell of a ride—almost as difficult as an Ironman, just in a different way. So, are you ready for take-off? Let's go!

PART III

10

THE DAILY LAUNCH

"Some people dream of success, while other people
get up every morning and make it happen."

~ Wayne Huizenga ~

For thousands of years, people have had the desire to fly.
Watching birds take flight and soar high into the air has
sparked the dream of flight in many people. It wasn't
until the early 1900s that the Wright brothers managed to
build rudimentary powered aircraft that could sustain flight
for short distances.

I like being around people who want to soar to new
heights, whether literally by learning to fly or figuratively by
reaching for their dreams, because they tend to have great
positive energy. I feel a kinship with them as I pursue my own
vision and dreams. Here in Part 3 are the most important
chapters of this book because this is where the "rubber hits
the road" and things get real.

If you want to achieve your dream lifestyle, accomplish
massive goals, and fulfill your vision, you've got to get serious

about focusing and doing the work it takes to make it happen. The kind of focus it takes is like piloting a plane. A airline pilot must learn how to maintain the right level of focus on a lot of different things at the same time, including operating the plane, maintaining radio contact with air traffic control, reading and interpret the weather, navigating to the destination, and a bunch of other things. Attention is a limited resource, so managing what you focus on is important. An effective morning routine like the one described in this chapter focuses attention on the most important things that help you level up.

The hard work required is the part many people don't want to hear, so I'm going to rely on a few famous people to help me make the point. Actor Will Smith puts it this way: "At the center of bringing any dream into fruition is self-discipline." Pro wrestler and actor Dwayne Johnson said, "Success at anything will always come down to this: Focus and effort, and we control both." Finally, entrepreneur and motivational speaker Jim Rhon said, "Discipline is the bridge between goals and accomplishment."

When you're working to obtain a helicopter pilot license, one of the things they drill into your head is the importance of performing a thorough preflight check before takeoff, just like airplane pilots. Many instructors impress the importance of the preflight checklist by telling stories about someone who got sloppy with their preflight check and ended up dying in a fiery crash. When it comes to the preflight checklist for a pilot, what's at stake is your very life, and the lives of any passengers who might also be on board—which is a great way to think about life.

Have you ever heard the phrase, *own your day, own your life*? If we can harness each day of our lives effectively, we can accomplish just about anything. Each day is a fresh chance to be the best version of yourself as possible. I've found the best way to ensure you own your whole day is by having an optimal morning routine and forming effective habits. You knew this was coming, right? Remember, those quotes above from Will Smith, Dwayne Johnson, and Jim Rohn come from hard-won experience, and they're talking about focus, discipline, and effort as *essential* to success. A morning checklist, what I'm calling the daily launch, is every bit as important as the preflight checklist is to a pilot. If we don't follow an optimal morning checklist, our dreams and vision are likely to remain unfulfilled.

What I'm going to share in this chapter is my own morning routine. It has been extremely effective for me. I'm not saying it's the way *yours* must be, but if you don't already have an optimal one, feel free to borrow mine as a starting point and then modify it to fit you better. In fact, customization to your unique needs makes perfect sense. After all, everyone has a different destination (a different vision), and the preflight checklist is going to be different depending on the destination, which dictates a surprising number of variables, not the least of which is having enough fuel to make it to your destination! This is why there's no such thing as a one-size-fits-all preflight checklist for a helicopter flight or your morning routine. First, I'm going to just list the elements of my 10-step morning routine, then you'll learn more about what each step includes and why. And yes, a truly effective morning checklist begins the night before!

MY MORNING ROUTINE: THE DAILY LAUNCH

- **Step 1: Preparing to Sleep**
  - Before going to bed, put phone on airplane mode and store it anywhere you want that is *not* in your bedroom.

- **Step 2: Daily Goal Setting**
  - Before falling asleep, write down your goals for the next day. Highlight the three most important goals.

- **Step 3: Waking Up Fresh and Grateful**
  - Upon waking, write down any dreams you remember while they're fresh.
  - Personal cleanse and refresh routine.
  - Think about three simple things for which you are grateful.

- **Step 4: Feeding Mind and Body**
  - Vision activation.
  - Hot lemon water.
  - Explosive push-ups until failure.

- **Step 5: Working Mind and Body**
  - Physical exercise/workout.
  - Listen to audiobook during workout.
  - Finish with 15-minute stretching session.

- **Step 6: Breathing and Reflecting with Intention**
  - Guided meditation focused on breathing.
  - Think about the intentions for the day, writing down whatever comes to mind.
  - Power intentions with affirmations.

- **Step 7: Framing the Day by Sharing Something Powerful**
  - Take something powerful (read, watch, or listen) and share it with others.

- **Step 8: Cold Shower and Healthy Breakfast**

- **Step 9: Informing the Day**
    - Read, watch, or listen to daily news.
    - Review goals for the day.
    - Review intentions for the day.

- **Step 10: Power the Day with Positivity**
    - Text positive messages to people for an uninterrupted 15 minutes.
    - Now, let's explore each step in greater detail to learn more about not only the *what* of each one but also the *why*.

STEP 1: PREPARING TO SLEEP

- Before going to bed, put phone on airplane mode or "do not disturb" and store it anywhere you want that is *not* in your bedroom.

The smartphones of today are powerful computing devices that allow anyone to accomplish more and more, right there in the palm of their hand. They are without doubt an incredible blessing, but they can also be a debilitating curse when not managed with some strict limits and boundaries. You can't own your morning let alone your whole day if you don't get enough sleep, or if you're constantly distracted by your phone.

This step of preparing to sleep is important, which is why I have an alarm set for 9:30 at night, which is my "time to unwind" alarm. When it goes off, I know it's time to put my phone into airplane mode because I don't want it to distract me from the rest of my evening routine. I do have a back-up emergency-only phone, and I give that number to a very small group of close family and friends so they know they can reach me if there's an emergency. In fact, my phone will stay in airplane mode until I'm done with the entire morning routine.

You don't have to get rid of your phone, but you do have to manage it wisely. I make use of my phone throughout my morning routine, but I keep it in airplane mode the entire time, and I also don't allow notifications from any app, which are a surefire path to constant distraction. And when it's time to sleep, the phone needs to be put away somewhere *outside* your bedroom.

"But Alvaro," I can hear you saying, "I use my phone as the alarm that wakes me up in the morning!" Fine, but it still doesn't need to be in your bedroom. Crank up the volume and have it just outside your bedroom. Or use an old-fashioned alarm clock. The point is to get plenty of high-quality sleep, and if your phone gets in the way of that, then you need to be intentional about managing it.

PRO-HACK

If getting out of bed in the morning is hard (snooze button syndrome), put your alarm far enough away from your bed that you've got to get out of bed to turn it off. Guess what? You're up!

Speaking of alarms, what time should you get up in the morning? That's up to you and depends on how long your morning routine is going to be and when you need to turn your attention to work. For me, I'm typically up sometime between and 4:30 and 5:30 in the morning. There are a surprising number of successful people who get up at 4:00 in the morning. Those who've made it a habit to get up that early note how there are very few distractions at that hour!

I went through a period when I did wake up at 4:00 in the morning and would immediately get on my phone and respond to all emails, texts, and notifications I had received. I thought this would show everyone around me how I was a really committed go-getter. As it turned out, I wasn't impressing anyone. In fact, all I was really doing was wasting time I could have spent on far more important things.

If you want to learn more about being more focused, meaning less distracted, I recommend reading (or listening to) a great book called *Indistractable: How to Control Your Attention and Choose Your Life* by Nir Eyal.

STEP 2: DAILY GOAL SETTING

- Before falling asleep, write down your goals for the next day. Highlight the three most important goals.

Keeping a journal handy is important because some of the elements of the morning routine involve writing things down— and here's the radical part—writing them by hand using a writing utensil (pen or pencil) on actual paper! Crazy, right? As you go through the steps of this morning routine, you'll notice it involves a variety of ways to process information that engage your mind in different ways using different senses. The more ways you process information, the more deeply they become embedded in your mind and body, which is key to making them habitual. You should also put these daily goals on your digital calendar or schedule for the next day. Why? As Tony Robbins has said, "If you talk about it, it's a dream. If you envision it, it's possible. If you schedule it, it's real."

Writing down your goals for the next day just before you go to bed is an important strategy because as you sleep, your brain will subconsciously be working on them, and you'll have an easier time accomplishing those goals the next day. I don't know who said, "What I write, I invite," but it's why I write down all my positive thoughts, ideas, and goals.

What are these daily goals? They are goals you can accomplish in one day because they are the smaller steps needed to reach larger goals. When you set a large goal, such as something you want to accomplish over the course of a year (or more), then you've got to break it down into smaller goals, such as monthly goals, that will get you there, and then even smaller goals such as weekly and daily goals. I call this "doing the math." Take any big goal you set and break it down into smaller and smaller goals, each one of which carries you along to achieving the goal within the desired timeframe. In other words, the daily goals you write down for the next day only make sense within a framework of larger goals you're working to achieve.

If you need to get a good handle on goal setting, I recommend reading (or listening to) *Your Best Year Ever: A 5-Step Plan for Achieving Your Most Important Goals* by Michael Hyatt and/or *Goals! How to Get Everything You Want—Faster Than You Ever Thought Possible* by Brian Tacy. They are both excellent resources for leveling up your goal-setting game to accomplish all your goals.

STEP 3: WAKING UP FRESH AND GRATEFUL

- Upon waking, write down any dreams you remember while they're fresh.
- Personal cleanse and refresh routine.
- Think about three simple things for which you are grateful.

When you first wake up in the morning, grab your journal and write down any dreams you remember before they slip away as they tend to do. This simple practice can give you all kinds of important insights if you also take time to reflect on what the dream you had might mean. In some cases, it might just be realizing why you had the dream, as in what triggered it.

In other cases, you may see a deeper and important meaning behind the dream. Make this a habit and before long you'll begin reaping unexpected rewards. If you want to be more intentional about this process, I recommend you read (or listen to) *The Power of Your Subconscious Mind* by Joseph Murphy.

The next element in this step is just whatever personal routine helps you feel clean, refreshed, and energized to tackle another day full of opportunities to make your dreams come true. This can include bathing/showering, skincare regimen, haircare, and so on. The final element in this step is to consciously think about three small, simple things for which you are grateful. Why small, simple things? Because it makes you more consciously inhabit the present moment. These are meant to be little things you might otherwise take for granted. You might think about how grateful you were to have a warm, soft blanket to cover you while you slept last night, or that you have a lemon in your fridge (you'll see why in the next step), and so on. Every day is different, and you'll be surprised what sorts of small things pop into your head for which you are truly grateful. Cultivating an attitude of gratitude in this way sets a positive tone for the rest of the day.

STEP 4: FEEDING YOUR MIND AND BODY

- Vision activation.
- Hot lemon water.
- Explosive push-ups until failure.

VISION ACTIVATION

This is one of the most important elements of all in the morning routine. Your vision is the big picture of what you want to achieve in life, and though it can and should change over time, you need to keep it in constantly in your mind so everything you do aligns with it. I have all the different pieces of my vision activation process saved in several different ways on my phone. They are first typed into my notes app and filed in different folders so I can read them. I have an audio recording of me reading them aloud so I can listen to them. I also have a whole slideshow movie of pictures that go along with the audio so I can see them represented as images.

What you want to do is run through all your Vision Activation content every morning during this step. If you need to multitask, you can be listening to it while you're doing the other elements in this step. Because I have accumulated a lot of content, this can take anywhere from twenty to thirty minutes during my morning routine. Below are the various components:

Vision

Remember, your vision is the big picture of what you want for your life, including your dream lifestyle. It should reflect all seven areas on the Wheel of Life, which are career, social, family, intellectual, physical, spiritual, and financial. Here's what mine was in the fall of 2022 when writing this book:

I am the CEO of the most recognized and successful multi-million-dollar real estate company and luxury media network in the world. This business brings an additional $10 million dollars revenue for me and my family every year. I travel the world with my family on our private jet to truly live, having unforgettable experiences, learning new cultures, doing business, and building new relationships. I own a beautiful house with ocean views in Miami where I live with my astonishing wife and children. I visit and spend quality time with my retired parents without them having to worry about any expenses.

I fly my own helicopter to adventures on the weekends, take the boat out to spend quality time with friends and family, and drive my white Audi R8 convertible to work each day. I work out almost every day, maintaining optimal health and fitness, which allows me to participate in super endurance races and challenges around the world. I skydive into beautiful destinations, luxury homes, and special events.

I speak five different languages. I have mastered the skills of leadership and sales. I am featured in multiple platforms as an icon in luxury real estate, lifestyle, and health. I have published multiple inspirational books that motivate individuals to become more successful and better in life. I speak at conferences in front of thousands of people to enlighten and change people's lives. I am a role model, mentor, and coach for those who need help, and I give back to the community every year while leaving a legacy that empowers positive change in the world.

My Why

To stay on track toward fulfilling your vision, you must remember the why behind all of it. In the My Why folder on my phone is the following:

To connect and help powerful mindsets make a positive impact, to support my parents, to travel the world with my future wife and children so we can learn new cultures and expand our network, to support my family in all their dreams and goals, to participate in the most challenging super endurance races carrying a meaningful purpose, to publish multiple inspirational books to motivate individuals to become better in life, to speak in front of thousands of people at conferences to enlighten and change their lives, to be a mentor and coach for those who need help, to give back to the community, and to leave a legacy that empowers positive change in the world.

What do you want to be known for? I want to be known for the inspirational self-help guidance and motivation I bring to others, as well as the valuable services, connections, and knowledge I offer within the luxury hospitality and real estate industry.

Why do I do what I do? Why real estate? To enhance people's lives through homes while connecting and building a community of individuals who inspire and want to make this world a better place. I originally started a luxury hospitality company because I love to travel, connect with people, and have unforgettable, life-changing experiences. I want to provide the same opportunities to those who share my passion for traveling and discovering all life has to offer.

Wheel of Life

You want to develop a variety of goals in each area of the Wheel of Life that over time you turn into habits and do them automatically. The reason making these kinds of goals habitual is so important is because of the *compound effect*. Do you remember learning about compound interest? It's why starting to save for retirement while you're still young makes so much sense. In year one you earn the simple interest on the principal investment, but in year two you earn interest on the principal as well as interest on the interest earned from year one if you keep it invested. Over the course of many years, you end up with a *lot* more money than if you just held your savings in cash and didn't invest it in something that earns compound interest.

Find out more about this concept as applied to goals and habits by reading (or listening to) *The Compound Effect: Jumpstart Your Income, Your Life, Your Success* by Darren Hardy. He makes the powerful point that you'll never change your life until you start changing things you do daily. The secret of success is found in your daily routine. In fact, he recommends turning your life goals into daily habits. When you apply these ideas to your Wheel of Life goals and they become habits, imagine the rewards you'll reap as you keep these practices up for years! Here are mine:

- **Career**
  - o Connect with ten new companies/individuals related to the business on a daily basis.
  - o Create valuable content daily and share it with my audience.
  - o Send daily updates to my database.
  - o Pitch my services/products to at least ten people every day.
  - o Achieve daily goals.

- **Social**
  - o Join five events (Gatherings, IG Live, Zoom panel, etc.) per week.
  - o Text or call ten friends a week.
  - o Contact ten old friends per week.

- **Family**
  - o Text or call all my brothers, sisters, and parents at least once a week.
  - o Text or call other extended family members at least once a month.
  - o Offer genuine help on each call I have with any family member.

- **Intellectual**
  - o Read or listen to two new books per week.
  - o Daily research about news and techniques related to my field.
  - o Read the news every day.
  - o Attend or watch a conference or mastermind every week.

- **Physical**
  - Work out at 5:30 am at least three times a week.
  - Work out through sports at least five times a week.
  - Run 26 miles each week.
  - Ride 100 miles on a bicycle each week.

- **Spiritual**
  - Once a week (morning/afternoon/night) for myself.
  - Do 5–10 minutes of guided meditation daily.
  - Write down three things every day for which I am grateful.

- **Financial**
  - Close five deals a week.
  - Do one activity daily that makes money.
  - Increase my net worth by 1% each week.

PRO-HACK

Forming new, more effective habits can be difficult. Get effective help by using a good habit app such as HabitShare (there are others) to measure, track, and hold yourself accountable as you form new habits.

Main Values

Keeping your core values front-and-center each day, which makes this component of Vision Activation as important as any other. Have you committed to core values in both your personal and professional life? Do you have words of toughness that make you feel confident and able to tackle any challenge? How about words that describe how you'll feel when you achieve each aspect of your vision or accomplish a massive goal?

Personal
Honesty
Loyalty
Passion
Humility
Empathy
Empowerment

Words of Toughness
Resilience
Relentless
Stamina
Determination
Focus
Perseverance

Business
Connected
Inspirational
Result-Oriented
Overdelivering
Beautiful Success

Words of Accomplishment
Satisfied
Fulfilled
Happy
Confident
Loved
Unstoppable
Strong
Human
Inspirational
Empowering

Growth Mindset

Your mindset is one of the most important things you can shape from one that isn't serving you well to one that fosters growth in all areas of life and drives forward momentum. This is the growth mindset. I use a number or reminders related to the growth mindset and incorporate them into my morning routine, including the following:

- Change fixed mindset to growth mindset.
- Remind yourself about accountability and ask the question of how to make your goals, dreams, and vision a reality.
- Combine intellect and passion to take yourself to the next level.
- Think like a shark, act like a shark, and behave like a shark.
- Failure and pain are temporary conditions.
- Ask yourself if you are taking enough risks.
- Position yourself for greatness by both attraction and action. Where you position your thoughts and actions is where your life is created.
- If you believe it, you will see it. Manifest the reality you want by visualizing. Be the change you want to see in the world.
- Read and learn daily news related to your field and interests.
- Create a business that fuels your passion.
- Visualize the lifestyle you want and assess whether your current "vehicle" can get you there.
- Everyone dies, but not everyone lives. Live full, die empty.

Massive Goals

If you don't set big goals, you can't achieve big things. A quote often attributed to Michelangelo, but which cannot be verified as something he ever said is "The greatest danger for most of us is not that our aim is too high and we miss it but that it is too low and we reach it." I think too many people limit themselves by dreaming too small. I encourage everyone to dream big and set ever-bigger goals. Some people call them "stretch goals" while others call them BHAGs (big hairy audacious goals). I call them massive goals, and here are some of mine:

- Make it onto the *Forbes* 30 under 30 list.
- Receive a one-million-dollar check.
- Skydive into an open house at our top exclusive property in Miami.
- Produce a luxury real estate television show.
- Host a conference in the luxury space attended by more than 10,000 people.
- Become the most recognized, successful real estate company and luxury network in the world.
- Develop a building/hotel.
- Create my own endurance challenge (The Luxury Path—a cross-country bike ride with stops at the most expensive homes in the country).
- Climb Mount Everest—the highest point on Earth.
- Complete the Marathon des Sables—the toughest footrace in the world.
- Be featured on the cover of Men's Health Magazine.
- Become a best-selling author.

Impact of Achieving Massive Goals:
- Set myself apart from everyone else.
- Invest more into the company, travel, and networking.

- A long-lasting first impression on the world.
- Overall legacy, success, and unlocking new connections and opportunities.
- Set the foundation for a long-lasting legacy in real estate.
- Bring exposure, inspiration, and education to both worlds of real estate and fitness.
- Empower and educate a community while making an impact on society.

Kryptonite (things to avoid):
- Comfort.
- Unmotivated and/or negative people.
- Distractions.

Relationships Vision

Something I've focused on more recently is being intentional about identifying people with whom I want to forge a connection. Something I've learned repeatedly over the years is the critical importance of building relationships with the right people. I make this intentional by identifying specific individuals I want to build a relationship with, and I maintain a list of them for each area on the Wheel of Life. These lists are long, so I won't reproduce them here, but you get the idea.

Habits

Here's the H-word again because you must not underestimate the massive benefits you can reap from forming effective habits. I keep a list of habits I've either already successfully adopted or am working on adopting. It is a very long list, so rather than listing them all here, you'll find them at the back of the book in Appendix: Habits to Level Up. Go through the list and select the ones that sound like good candidates for you to adopt.

A good tip here to keep in mind is the idea of "stacking" habits to adopt and integrate new ones. Most people already have a kind of morning routine in place to some extent, so find places within it where you can insert a new habit that makes sense in the overall sequence. Keep stacking habits in this way and your daily launch will become increasingly effective over time. Habits that aren't getting results can be removed and then you can insert a new one into the stack. The morning routine outlined here is an accumulation and evolution of stacking habits over several years.

HOT LEMON WATER

Every morning I drink a cup of hot water with plenty of lemon in it. Why? It offers a surprising number of health benefits. Lemon is an alkaline food that helps keep your body's pH level balanced. It's also a good detoxification practice as it literally wakes up your liver and flushes out toxins. This simple beverage also has big digestive benefits as it stimulates the gastrointestinal tract to more effectively absorb nutrients throughout the day.

PRO-HACK

Add things to your hot lemon water that would be especially beneficial for *you*, such as ginger for its anti-inflammatory and antioxidant properties, or pink sea salt if you need to retain water because of intense physical workouts or endurance activities.

EXPLOSIVE PUSH-UPS TO FAILURE

This element of Step 4 in my morning routine is meant to get the blood pumping, which is good for your brain, and build muscles while doing it. You could substitute any number of physical activities that are good fit for you.

STEP 5: WORKING YOUR MIND AND BODY

- Physical exercise/workout.
- Listen to audiobook during workout.
- Finish with 15-minute stretching session.

This step in the morning routine is focused on the health of your body and your mind. Decide on different kinds of physical workouts and exercise routines that best suit you but use this time effectively by also giving your mind a workout through listening to an audiobook with content that will help you be better in some way, whether related to your career or your personal life. A morning physical workout is key because it makes your brain more effective. Studies have shown that students who have gym class during their first period in school get better grades.

STEP 6: BREATHING AND REFLECTING WITH INTENTION

- Guided meditation focused on breathing.
- Think about the intentions for the day, writing down whatever comes to mind.
- Power intentions with affirmations.

GUIDED BREATH MEDITATION

This step is all about fully inhabiting the present moment and then setting your intentions for the day. Meditative breathing is the most effective way I've found to ground myself in the present moment and doing it in the morning is important because this is when your brain's creative power is at its maximum. I use guided meditations that are focused on breathing, and there are different types of breathing you can focus on depending on your needs. This doesn't have to be a long session either. I do a guided meditation focused on breathing for about ten minutes during this step, using an app on my phone called Meditation. There are quite a few meditation apps out there, so find the one that's right for you.

INTENTION JOURNALING

Grab your journal and spend a little time thinking about intentions for your day and write down whatever comes to mind, which may include not just positive items but also constructive items to address, such as pain points and areas in your life you know need improvement.

AFFIRMATIONS

Setting great intentions for the day is fine, but if you want to power them up to happen, turn them into positive affirmations that start with "I can..." "I will..." "I am..." and so on. These affirmations will help you fulfill your intentions for the day.

STEP 7: FRAMING THE DAY BY SHARING SOMETHING POWERFUL

- Take something powerful (read, watch, or listen) and share it with others.

If you're serious about CNEI (constant, never-ending improvement), which you should be since it's one of the most effective ways to stay on track as you make your way toward your vision, this one will be easy. I have a whole collection of different things I have found to be powerful, whether it's something I read in a book, a video I saw, an online post from someone else that impacted me in a good way, and so on. I take one of these powerful items and I share it online. Remember, my phone is still on airplane mode, so it won't send until I bring my phone back online, but it's all ready to go. If you don't have a collection of powerful items to draw on, find your own sources. There are all kinds of motivational, inspirational website and YouTube channels out there that offer plenty of powerful material.

This step is a win-win for you and the people you share it with. For you, you'll re-experience what was powerful about the item, which will boost your motivation. Remember, while motivation gets you started, it is discipline that keeps you going. You need both.

STEP 8: COLD SHOWER AND HEALTHY BREAKFAST

Why a cold shower? The health benefits are huge, believe it or not. I know you're cringing at the idea of a cold shower but trust me when I say if you can muster the willpower to do it on a regular basis, you'll become a loyal fan. It's a mild form of oxidative stress you can adapt to, and when you do, you'll find you deal with stress and other emotional challenges much more easily than before because you've "hardened" yourself (like building up callouses from manual labor). This simple body hardening hack helps you stay calm, cool, and collected no matter what life throws at you.

Cold showers stimulate you and make you alert, are better for both your skin and your hair, improves circulation, increases both testosterone and fertility, boosts your immune system because of the "cold shock proteins" generated, and speeds up muscle recovery after intense workouts. A cold shower also stimulates the production of endorphins that can reduce depressive symptoms and generally elevate your mood.

As for a healthy breakfast, it's important to take in the right nutrients early in the day, and I'll have more to say about diet in chapter 12, which focuses on health.

STEP 9: INFORMING THE DAY

- Read, watch, or listen to daily news.
- Review goals for the day.
- Review intentions for the day.

Don't get sucked into the news but do read (or listen or watch) just enough so you know what's happening in the world and won't appear to be "out of the loop" when interacting with people throughout the day. I limit this element to 15 minutes. Notice there's a defined limit here! Have you heard of Parkinson's Law? It says, "Work expands so as to fill the time available for its completion." For me, this means if you don't have a clear start time and finish time for a task, it's going to drag on longer than it needs to. This is an important practice when it comes to time management.

PRO-HACK

Use the Pomodoro Technique throughout your day. It's one of the best time management tools and productivity hacks out there. You'll wonder how you ever survived without it!

Because you're nearing the end of the morning routine and want to hit the ground running for the rest of your day, now is the time to quickly review both your goals and intentions for the day (including affirmations). Then you're ready for the next and final step of the daily launch.

STEP 10: POWER THE DAY WITH POSITIVITY

- Text positive messages to people for an uninterrupted 15 minutes.

It's so important to end your morning routine with something positive, which is why this last step is continuous texting for 15 uninterrupted minutes. Remember, your phone should still be in airplane mode, so you're entering the messages and then they will send when you bring your phone back online. What I do is work my way down through my contacts list, writing each a positive text message (or audio message or video message) in which I express my gratitude to them for whatever role they have played or are playing in my life—usually combined with a specific memory about them. This is another "attitude of gratitude" action that's important because having gratitude and not expressing it is like wrapping up a lovely gift and never giving it!

* * * * *

Now that you've seen the details of my morning routine, you may be thinking, "Gosh, Alvaro, this seems really complicated." Yes, but trust me when I say it's worth it! Your morning routine is the preflight checklist for your day. Only after completing it will you be ready to optimize your day and make your dreams come true. Like a helicopter pilot, you've got to remember what's at stake with the checklist, which is your life. That's how important an effective morning routine is for leveling up to your dream life. You also need to fuel and maintain a helicopter to get peak performance out of it. In the same way, you've got to fuel and maintain the vehicle you've chosen that will carry you to your dream life, which is what the next chapter is all about.

11

RELATIONSHIPS TO FUEL YOUR VEHICLE

"I believe that you can get everything in life you want
if you will just help enough other people
get what they want."

~ Zig Ziglar ~

The previous chapter was all about building a powerful morning routine to launch each day with positive energy and forward momentum toward our vision. But what's the vehicle that will get you there? For many people it's their career that becomes the vehicle, which can work out great if you're passionate about it. The business I established has been my primary vehicle and being in luxury real estate aligns well with my life vision and lets me lean into my passions. Whatever vehicle you choose, accelerate it by putting in the best fuel possible, which is often *relationships*.

When you look the list of Habits to Level Up in the appendix, notice how many of them have to do with how you relate to people and interact with them. More than a quarter of them are about relationships! Relationships are always the key to any business, but if you think about it, relationships are essential to every area on The Wheel of Life. We would all be better off if we thought of our *network* as our *net worth*. Although the word "networking" has fallen somewhat out of favor because of overuse, all networking has ever really meant is building relationships. Simply put, anyone who isn't good at building relationships has a big obstacle to overcome. The good news is that stacking up the right habits can make relationship building one of your superpowers. Here are some starting points:

Positive Energy: Back in Chapter 7 I mentioned how *positive energy is the current currency for professional and personal success.* This relates to the whole idea of the law of attraction, meaning what you put out into the world is what you'll get back, so bring as much positive energy to every interaction you have with people as possible. Enthusiasm can and will generate all kinds of opportunities. This is why one of the habits you'll find in the appendix is this: Smile! You are stronger when you smile because smiling is positive energy. Another one is to be like a tree. Why? Trees breathe in carbon dioxide, which for humans is air pollution, and exhale the life-giving oxygen we need. So be like a tree—when people are throwing negativity at you, inhale it and then exhale positivity. Be a beacon of light in a world that already has way too much darkness and negativity in it and you'll attract people to you. Most everyone wants to be around that positive energy.

Adding Value: Approach every new and existing relationship with being determined to bring value to the other person. Zig Ziglar, the well-known author, salesman, and motivational speaker, had the right idea in the quote at the top of this chapter—helping other people get what they want will help you get what you want. It's the law of attraction again, just in a slightly different form. Approaching people with a mindset of what you want to get from them isn't about adding value, it's about extracting value from the other person. It's not an effective way to build the kind of relationships you need to level up. Below are a few habits that align with a value-added approach to building relationships:

- Start conversations by asking questions to learn what someone wants and identify ways to bring them value.
- Build and nurture relationships every day, not only when you need them.
- Ask your partner every morning: "What can I help you with today?"
- Learn quickly what makes a person tick and cater to that as soon as possible.
- To influence people, talk about what they want and show them how to get it.
- Give, give, give, and then ask.

Effective Delegation: Taking the time to build great relationships is what helps anyone become more effective at delegation. Fulfilling a big life vision is going to be impossible if *you* try to do everything related to fueling, maintaining, and operating your vehicle. One of my older brothers was a professional racecar driver. In the middle of a race when his car needed attention, did he pull off to the side and get out of the car to fuel it or change a tire? Of course not! He pulled into a pitstop where there was a whole team of people ready and waiting to do everything for him so he could get back onto the track in as little time as possible. If you've never seen a Formula 1 race, you should check it out sometime. There are *twenty* people on an F1 pit crew, and it's amazing to see how much they accomplish in a matter of seconds.

My business is in the luxury real estate field, but that doesn't mean I'm out there every day showing homes to clients. On the contrary, when I meet someone who is looking to sell a luxury property or a serious buyer looking to purchase one, I will often refer them or work with someone in my network who I know and can trust to get the job done. Who I refer a client to is something that must be carefully considered. It requires learning enough about the client and knowing who aligns best with them on multiple levels and across various interests. This is not just any referral process, it's a very intentional and carefully vetted undertaking. When I make excellent matches, it's a triple-win where the client gets what they want, my colleague makes a great sale, and I get a substantial referral fee.

Scaling up this network is what resulted in establishing the SLG Network. It's an exclusive, invitation-only group of industry leaders passionate about luxury real estate. We've assembled an incredible powerhouse network of successful players that includes agents, brokers, developers, architects, interior designers, influencers, and marketers. We bring together the right players to the right projects so everyone wins.

Building a Network: When the SLG Members Network was being developed, it was important to build it up into a robust network as quickly as possible, so I was looking for a way to leverage other people's audiences (OPAs). This was when the global pandemic was in full force, and I began to wonder how other people in luxury space were doing during such difficult times. As I reached out and talked to some of the key players I knew, I was so impressed with their stories of how they were managing things. I realized others in the industry would probably love to hear these inspiring stories, so I started up an interview series to feature these leaders. These started out as simple Instagram live interviews and quickly morphed into a full-blown ongoing podcast called SLG Meetups.

Over the past couple years, I've interviewed hundreds of people in the luxury space, and it has been such a rewarding project for everyone involved. I learned so much from these people during our conversations, and each one brought the relationship with them to a whole new and deeper level, which inevitably leads to all kinds of great opportunities. The interviewees were getting great exposure, so they were happy. And the people who were listening and watching the interviews were getting fantastic insider information. Meanwhile, I was getting great exposure for both my personal brand and for SLG. Over time, the compound effect of SLG Meetups and tapping into OPAs has been massive.

One of the reasons the podcast has become so successful is because my primary motivation isn't about me or what I'm doing. Instead, it's about the person I'm interviewing. It's always better to put the other person first and make it about them, not you. The exposure you end up getting out of it is like the icing on a win-win cake. For this kind of collaboration to work, it's important to know how to ask great questions. This is why one of the habits in the appendix is *learn how to ask the good questions*. As Tony Robbins put it, "Successful people ask better questions, and as a result, they get better answers." And then, of course, it's important to *listen* to the answers.

What about you? As you begin developing your own powerhouse network in whatever you're passionate about, keep your eyes open for opportunities to meet, bring value, and work with them in some capacity. When you focus on adding value, you'll be surprised how quickly new collaborations emerge that will benefit everyone.

Collaboration as Social Currency: In the same way positive energy is a powerful social currency, so is collaboration. The

SLG Meetups I mentioned above worked out so well because it was beneficial for everyone involved. The same has been true of the SLG Network. When people see on social media how I was attending red-carpet events or staying in the most luxurious accommodations in a jetsetter destination, it's not because I'm spending huge resources to do those things. Instead, it means a lot of careful planning has gone into bringing together the right collaborations, which will lead to these amazing opportunities.

Always be on the lookout for win-win collaborations. They're out there, you've just got to stay hungry for them. Again, they're more likely to arise when your approach to building relationships is one of bringing value rather than trying to extract it. Make a habit of asking yourself, "Who can I help today?"

Role Models: Whatever field you may be in, always find and keep role models in mind. Study the key players you admire most, learn about their journey to success. If they come out with a book, buy it and read it. Then go even further and think in terms of how you might be able to start building a real relationship with them. Give them a shout-out on your social media to show your appreciation, and comment in their social media how much you enjoyed the content. These may seem like small things to do, but you'd be surprised how often this can lead to additional interactions and even relationships with them.

In Chapter 10 I mentioned developing what I call a "relationships vision" for each area on the Wheel of Life, listing the key players and role models I want to work with in some way, and I encourage everyone to do the same. Sometimes even the smallest things can become opportunities to go deeper with a relationship. Entrepreneur, author, and rapper Jesse Itzler is a person I admire. I bought a sun visor from one of his companies and liked it enough that I did a little social media post about it with a shout-out to him. He saw it, checked out my social media, and he reached out to me—which opened a new door of exciting opportunities ahead. When you get a chance to interact with one of your role models does come up, find ways to bring them value and you could end up having great relationships with people you previously thought were far beyond your reach.

Carpe Diem: Seize the day! After you've met a new, interesting person and interacted with them, follow-up immediately with an idea or something else that brings value. Don't wait until the next week or the next day. Don't even wait until you get home after the event where you met the person. Literally do a follow-up with them as you're walking away. These immediate follow-ups are also a good opportunity to go the extra mile and do something different. Don't just send a text message or an email. Send your follow-up as a selfie video or audio message. It will have far more impact than text or email. And it's not just a thank-you note. Make sure it has an idea or some other content with momentum that will lead to an action of some sort.

Speaking of seizing the day, another great habit to adopt is the thirty-second rule, although this one isn't about building relationships. Whenever you read something, or listen to something, or attend an event, presentation, meeting, or have some kind of experience, take thirty seconds to right down the most important takeaways that come to mind. Make this a habit and it will become one of your most valuable superpowers because it trains your mind to always latch onto the most important points from everything you do.

Be an Outlier: In terms of personal branding and professional networking, few things are more important than differentiation. Being different from everyone else in your field is a surefire way to accelerate exposure. Be the more interesting person in a room an others will be naturally attracted to you, right? Find the ways you are or can become a unique outlier and capitalize on it. Lots of people are in the luxury real estate space, especially in Miami, but very few of them are skydivers, and even fewer of them do Ironman, travel the world and attend red carpet events, or have a helicopter pilot license. I don't mention these things to brag about them, but to point out how having unique passions that differentiate yourself in a positive way in your field is pure gold. It will draw people to you on the lifestyle level, which is always a powerful attractor.

It's so much more enjoyable to connect with people on shared interests and passions rather than just thinking about the business side of the relationship. I do show homes to clients when I can see we are well aligned. It's also a lot of fun to go the extra mile in showing a home. I never just ask the client to meet me at the home. There's no deeper connection to be made by doing that (and not much fun either). Instead, it will be a whole carefully curated experience. It's so much more satisfying to do it this way, and it will make such a strong first impression, which is always important. With my helicopter pilot license, I can take a client on an aerial tour of Miami with pauses over the homes we will then look at in-person on the ground afterwards. You only get to make a first impression once, so make the most of it!

If I know the client is into healthy living and fitness as much as I am, maybe I'll invite them to go on a morning run with me, and the destination of the run will be the home I want to show them. And maybe there will be a super-healthy breakfast prepared by a great chef on-site ready and waiting for us on the terrace with an ocean view. Meanwhile, the time spent during the run and the meal is more time to go deeper with the client, leveling up the relationship even before we do the grand tour of the home. Always be willing to go the extra mile to go deeper and build stronger relationships. And if you really want to jumpstart a deeper connection with someone, take them skydiving. Trust me, it works!

Treating People Right: To conclude this chapter, there are several habits for leveling up that are surprisingly simple and yet profoundly impactful. They are about how to treat other people, which is incredibly important in terms of building meaningful relationships. Everyone knows the basic golden rule of treating others the way you want to be treated. Below are ten related habits we would all do well to keep in mind for building positive, productive relationships with all our fellow human beings:

- Make people feel significant and recognized for their accomplishments.
- Treat everyone equally regardless of their status or relationship to you.
- Don't talk about someone unless they are in the room with you (avoid gossip).
- Make the person you are talking to feel empowered (give compliments).
- Create and foster unity by approaching everyone with "us/we" instead of "you/I."
- Make everyone in a conversation feel important.
- Compassion creates connection, so be compassionate with others (and yourself).
- Always show up for those who are suffering or in need.
- Listen when someone is talking to you.
- Have empathy and look at things from the other person's point of view.

Think about how wonderfully different the world would be if everyone could agree to adopt those ten habits in their personal and professional lives. Anyone can adopt the kinds of positive relationship-building habits mentioned throughout this chapter and experience how they can accelerate leveling up. But there's one last vehicle to help carry you toward your vision that we need to talk about in the next and final chapter, and it is your health!

12

HEALTH IS WEALTH

"A man too busy to take care of his health is like
a mechanic too busy to take care of his tools."

~ Spanish Proverb ~

Throughout this book, you've read about having a vehicle fueled by passion and sometimes pain to carry you toward the vision of your dream life. For me, the vehicle has been the business I started, Super Luxury Group. But now it's time to take a deeper look into the ultimate vehicle of all: your health. And I mean all your health, including your body, your mind, and your spirit. In the fast-paced world of today, it's all too easy to forget how health is our true wealth. Without health, none of our dreams will matter because we either won't live long enough to make them come true or won't be able to enjoy them. Someone once said, "A healthy person has a thousand wishes, a sick person has only one," which is to be well. In this final chapter, I'll share my thoughts and some of the tools I use to maintain a healthy personal vehicle.

The best place to start is always with the basics. First and foremost is self-awareness and being honest with yourself. Do you feel great all the time? If not, why not? Examine your habits! Most people have a pretty good idea of things they do or don't do that get in the way of being healthy, whether it's a poor diet, not getting enough sleep, lack of exercise, or obvious bad habits like smoking, drinking, and so on. Bad habits are kryptonite that rob you of your superpowers.

If it's not difficult to see where improvements could be made to become healthier, then what is it that holds people back from making positive changes? In many cases, it is a matter of motivation. In other cases, finding out the root causes behind what's keeping people from feeling great may require deeper exploration and help from health professionals.

Overcoming the inertia to eliminate bad habits and adopt healthier ones isn't easy. If it was easy, everyone would be optimizing their health. What it takes is a powerful vision to which you are fully committed. This is why developing a vision for your life is so important and why, once you've created it, keeping it front-and-center on a daily basis is critical. It's a big part of why the morning routine you read about in Chapter 10 (The Daily Launch) is essential. Your "Why" also comes into play here. Both your vision and your why can be strong motivators.

Here's a hack that can help: Wherever you have your alarm set up to get you up in the morning (remember, it should be far enough away from your bed that you have to get up to go turn it off), have a picture there of something from your vision or your why so as you turn off the alarm, you're also seeing something that is incredibly important to you. It is a reminder of what's at stake and will help motivate you for your morning routine and healthier habits.

Fear also plays a big role in holding people back from making positive changes in their life. Whether it's fear of failure, fear of rejection, fear of being judged, and so on, fear has a way of stopping people from ever getting started or killing momentum when they do try. Fear happens, but the key is what you do once you feel it. Courage means taking actions despite the fear. Again, have your vision and your why ready to help you muster the courage you need to act even when fear tries to stop you.

PRO-HACK

Use the 21-day challenge approach to introduce a new healthier habit. If you make it to day 21, you'll have the momentum you need to make it permanent.

The 21-day challenge approach is a great hack for adopting new habits, which came from plastic surgeon Maxwell Maltz back in the 1950s. He noticed it seemed to take his patients around 21 days to adjust to their new post-surgery normal. Applying the rule more broadly in his 1960 book *Psycho-Cybernetics*, what he said was that establishing a new habit or norm is going to take at least 21 days. Self-help gurus have been using this idea ever since, although it should be noted Maltz said it would take *at least* 21 days for a new habit to become settled. It's not like you hit day 21 and you're cured. It means if you can get to the 21-day mark, then you've got enough momentum to carry you through to making it a permanent change. How long it takes for a habit to become fully permanent is going to vary from person to person. Research has shown the average to be around 66 days for the brain's neural network to make a new habit automatic.

Now, let's get into some details about healthier living and the tools that can help you optimize the health of your body, mind, and spirit.

YOUR BODY: PHYSICAL HEALTH

Think of your home, the place where you live, as a sacred temple. You don't want to let anything in that would harm your health. Also think of your body as another sacred temple, and once again don't put anything in it or on it that will harm your health. As you eliminate the things you know aren't healthy, then you can start paying more attention to optimizing the things that have the greatest impact on your physical health: Eating, drinking, breathing, sleeping, and exercising.

OPTIMAL EATING

Getting the right nutrients into your body is one of the most impactful things you can do on the journey to optimal health. But here's the thing: Like with so many things in life, everyone is unique and different, which means the specific diet you should be on ought to be customized to meet your unique needs. Yes, there are broad approaches to eating healthier that will probably be beneficial for nearly anyone (less sugar, fewer highly processed foods, more vegetables and fruit, and so on), but it makes sense to go further and find out what *your* body specifically needs and tailor your diet and/or supplements to meet those needs.

The best way to find out what *your* body needs in terms of nutrition is through several different tests, including a blood test, a gene test, and gut test. Yes, these tests do come at a cost, but the knowledge they provide for optimizing your health will be truly priceless. Considering what's at stake (your health), the money spent is a very small investment with a huge return if you make adjustments to your habits based on what you learn.

Gene Test: Specifically, a methylation test. It gives you a comprehensive look at your overall health and what enzymes are affected by your genetic makeup. It basically tells you if your body is running the way it should. This gives you great insights into what you can do to optimize your health. I had mine done by a company called 10X Health System.

Blood Test: I also had this done through 10X Health System. The test looks at something like 64 different biomarkers to give you an even more in-depth look at why you feel the way you do health-wise, as well as what you can start doing immediately to optimize your health based on the results. You'll find out if your body is deficient in various areas and how you can resolve imbalances with changes to your diet and/or supplements.

Gut Test: There's rising awareness of how important your "gut flora" is to better health. For this one, there are several different companies that offer a gut intelligence test—an analysis of your gut microbiome that reveals not only what you need more of in terms of nutrients, but also what your superfoods are and what foods you should specifically avoid based on your unique gut microbiome.

It's also worth having some allergen testing done to find out what you might be allergic to so you can eliminate those from your diet or your environment. Even being just slightly allergic to something can keep you from feeling optimally healthy.

You've probably also heard about inflammation being something that can cause all kinds of issues in the human body. Chronic low-grade inflammation over time can cause serious health problems, including depression, arthritis, heart disease, Alzheimer's disease, and cancer. Foods that make inflammation worse include red meat, refined carbohydrates (think white bread, muffins, pastries, and so on), fried foods, and sugary drinks. Anti-inflammatory foods include tart cherries, fatty fish, olive oil, ginger, turmeric, garlic, onions, whole grains, dark leafy greens, nuts, berries, citrus fruits, tomatoes, and tea. Tomatoes had to come off my list, however, because the gut test told me my system does not like tomatoes and I should avoid them.

The insights and guidance you receive from the various tests mentioned above are invaluable to understanding what you should be feeding your body if you want to see truly astonishing improvements in your overall health and wellbeing.

OPTIMAL HYDRATION

By now, most people have at least some awareness of how important it is to keep your body hydrated. After all, the average human body is more than 60% water! You'll see different numbers thrown around in this regard because it differs with age (infants are 80% water when born) and body type (lean body mass carries way more water than body fat), but the average is 60%. Any time that percentage drops below 60%, all body systems suffer. So yes, drinking water is critical. I aim for a gallon a day because I'm very physically active. It's a nice round goal, though, from which anyone would benefit.

PRO-HACK

Drink alkalinized (higher pH) water to counteract too much acidity in your body.

What fewer people know is that the *kind* of water you drink can also make a difference, and here is where there is an opportunity to go further than most. Most people think water is water, right? Well, let's talk about pH, which is a scale that measures acidity on a scale of 0–14. A pH level of 7 is considered neutral, while a pH level above 7 is considered alkaline (also called "basic"). What's considered a normal pH level for your blood is 7.35–7.45. Where most people get into trouble is when their pH level is too acidic, meaning the pH level is lower than it should be. Drinking higher-pH (alkaline) water can help your body get back to a better pH level and improve digestion, sleep, rehydration after intense exercise, and other benefits. I'm a fan of high-pH water. There are lots of alkaline water machines options out there nowadays for home use. The brand of machine I use is Kangen, a company that makes several different models depending on your needs.

Speaking of water, remember how I mentioned cold showers back in Chapter 10? If you really want to get the most benefit out of cold-water therapy, also called cold hydrotherapy, take a regular ice bath! I know, you're thinking I've really gone off the deep end, right? And yet the health benefits are huge. There are other ways to get cold hydrotherapy that don't involve filling your bathtub with ice. And it only takes a matter of minutes on a regular basis to reap all the benefits.

OPTIMAL SLEEP

Too many people think they can shortchange how much sleep they get without causing any harm, but nothing could be further from the truth. Adequate, high-quality sleep is essential to living your best and healthiest life. For me, I know I need a good seven hours of quality sleep to be fully functional and on point throughout the day. It's also important to realize being in bed for seven or eight hours doesn't mean you got the high-quality sleep you need. What the body needs is to cycle through the various stages of sleep several times in one night.

Stages 1 and 2 are light sleep and might make up as much of 50% of the sleep you get. Stage 3 is deep sleep and is super-important. It's the most rejuvenating and restorative sleep you can get and should be roughly 15–20% of your sleep. During this stage you're very still, relaxed, and hard to wake up. Your blood pressure drops while breathing and heart rate are steady. It is during deep sleep that your muscles repair and grow, your brain gets rid of toxins, and your immune system is refreshed. Deep sleep tends to happen earlier in the night. Some people purposely interrupt their deep sleep because that's when their brain is having their best ideas. Then comes Stage 4 of sleep, which is REM (rapid eye movement) and is important for dreaming, memory consolidation, and creativity. People tend to get more REM sleep during the latter half of the night. Increasing the quality of sleep is as easy as avoiding stimulants, heavy meals, and bright screens for a couple hours before going to bed, and make sure sleeping time is consistent.

PRO-HACK

Use a sleep tracker to monitor and achieve optimal sleep. The Oura ring and mobile app will give you the information you need to get as much high-quality sleep as you need each night.

The problem is that it can be hard to know whether you're getting quality sleep or not. If your sleep quality gradually degrades over time, you might not even realize it. This is when it can be helpful to find out more about your own unique sleep patterns and quality of sleep. You can do this either through a professional sleep clinic or by making use of a sleep tracking functionality like the Oura ring. It's very good at detecting the timing and duration of the different stages of sleep. For me, the Oura ring showed me how my body temperature was running too high during the night for optimal sleep, even though I didn't feel uncomfortably warm. I lowered the nighttime temperature just a bit and saw immediate improvement in the quality of my sleep, meaning waking up feeling more rested and refreshed.

OPTIMAL BREATHING

You've been breathing pretty much non-stop since the moment you were born. It's probably the most important thing we constantly do and yet rarely think about if ever. You can go weeks without eating, days without sleeping or drinking, but stop breathing and your life will end in a matter of minutes. Despite the necessity of breathing, most people don't stop to think about it and yet we should. There's a reason why so many religious and spiritual practices focus on breath. It's a wonderful mechanism through which to focus on the present moment and fully inhabiting it.

But in the same way most people don't think about what type of water they drink, they also don't tend to consider the air they're breathing. Polluted air is no good, obviously, but even clean air doesn't have as much oxygen in it as you might think. The minimum oxygen content needed in the air we breathe is 19.5%. The natural concentration of oxygen in air here on planet Earth is around 21%. Seems like we're cutting it kind of close there, doesn't it? But too much oxygen can also be problematic. A safe way to get more oxygen that can work wonders for your health is called mild hyperbaric oxygen therapy (mHBOT). It delivers optimal amounts of oxygen under pressure and literally improves everything, including sleep, energy, circulation, concentration, metabolism, healing, immune function, and so much more. Home systems are available, though they can be rather expensive.

OPTIMAL EXERCISE

You need to exercise! I'm not going to tell you what you should do or how you should do it, but you've got to be physically active to be healthy. Exercise releases a key hormone, dopamine, as well as the neurotransmitter serotonin. Both of these play an important role in regulating mood, which is why people who exercise experience less anxiety and depression. Because I was an athlete from childhood all the way through college, I was used to regular workouts and intense physical training. Since then, I have found myself drawn to increasingly more difficult and extreme challenges, such as the Ironman. Next year I'm going to start off by trying to complete the toughest footrace in the world called the Marathon de Sables, a six-day race covering 156 miles or the equivalent of six marathons in southern Morocco. Other exciting challenges are in the works that I'll post about on social media, so stay tuned! The reason I take on these challenges is because I'm fascinated by testing the limits of human performance.

All these health-optimizing practices and tools are interconnected across the basics of eating, drinking, breathing, sleeping, and exercising. Some might make improvements in just one area and still be very unhealthy in the other areas but making improvements in all areas is like turbocharging our health in unimaginable ways. Again, starting small by eliminating obvious bad habits and then stacking up healthier habits is the way to go. Adding just one new habit every 21 days to make sure the previous one has good momentum means adding around 17 new healthy habits in one year. This gradual approach rather than trying to tackle everything all at once is smart.

Success at improving physical health is all about measuring to track changes, otherwise we won't know if we're making progress. There are lots of fitness and health tracking devices and apps, so choose one that suits you. One thing I can say for sure: Getting serious about investing in your health will pay the greatest dividends of all because health is the ultimate wealth that matters more than any other.

YOUR MIND: HEALTHY MINDSETS

Self-awareness and presence are two important themes when it comes to a healthy mind. Fulfilling a vision and making dreams come true takes more than just wishing and hoping and dreaming. Taking action in the present moment to level up is the key. Moving forward in the present moment is paramount. Why is the present moment so important? Because when you think about it, it's all we have. Many people twist their minds up in knots with worry and anxiety about the future. Others get stuck in an endless loop of reliving past regrets. Don't get me wrong, I'm all for learning from past mistakes and making plans for the future. But what matters most is what we do in the *present* moment to apply the lessons learned from the past and the actions we take to make our dreams for the future come true. If we're not fully self-aware and present in the *now*, none of it will matter.

Every new day is an opportunity to take actions focused on accomplishing goals that keep us moving in the right direction. Each time we accomplish a goal, whether it's a small stepping-stone goal on the pathway of achieving a larger goal, or finally accomplishing a massive goal, we must never stop and think to ourselves, "I did it! I've arrived! Now I can take a break." If we do that, we run the risk of backsliding to a previous state. When you accomplish a goal, go ahead and celebrate but then *immediately* set a new goal that raises the bar even higher. Whatever you just accomplished is now a new baseline to use as a launching pad to level up beyond it. This might also require retooling your vision by dreaming even bigger, go further, reach higher, train harder, work smarter, and achieve more. Let's be *hungry* for what comes next!

Too many people achieve a goal and then backslide because they start to make excuses. They think they've accomplished something and can rest on their laurels. This is a surefire way to kill all their momentum and get stuck where they're at. The problem with this is that if we're not growing, then we're dying. If we're not moving forward with purpose and determination, then life is passing us by. If we're not leveling up, then we're falling back to a previous state. Don't make excuses. Instead, set new goals and start acting on them. Excuses are *lies*. Return to your vision and your why and get fired up to keep going!

We must each own our individual journey and be 100% accountable for becoming the hero of our own stories. Don't rely on others or expect others to fill in the gaps. This doesn't mean we don't ever accept help or delegate responsibility because trust me when I say we all need to do both of those. What I mean is we must each always be sure we are doing everything in our own power to move forward. If you're not where you want to be, then it's time to take an introspective look at what role you have played in being where you're at.

This is when self-awareness and being honest with ourselves is critical. We must avoid making excuses or blaming others for our circumstances. When we lie to ourselves by making excuses or pointing the finger at others or blaming circumstances, we are giving up our own power and agency to control what happens next. We can't control others, and many circumstances are also beyond our control, but we can always be in control of ourselves and what we do next. That's what I mean by being 100% accountable for everything in your life. It's up to each of us to figure out what we each need to do differently to get the desired results, which in turn requires the right mindset.

Jumpstarting what I call a mindset reset to level up can be as easy as paying closer attention to the words we speak. Words are powerful, and sometimes an inner voice will tell us negative things that can wreck our mindset. Without realizing it we may start to believe that inner voice telling us how we can't do it, and suddenly doubts and fears begin holding us back. This is when we can squash any negative self-talk by changing up our words, such as the following:

From IF to WHEN
From BUT to AND
From COST to INVESTMENT
From EXPENSIVE to PREMIUM
From PROBLEM to CHALLENGE
From STRESSED to CONCERNED
From FEAR to EXCITEMENT

I also want to say something about depression. When people look at my social media or spend time with me in person, I'm known as a happy, can-do, positive kind of guy. In fact, I work hard at being that person. But it doesn't mean everything is always rainbows and unicorns. We all go through dark times, me included. There will surely be dark times ahead of us as well. What I can say is that I've seen far more people than I care to admit reach incredible success in their lives and still fall prey to depression despite their achievements. Being among young elite athletes who were on track to become world class professionals, I saw first-hand how the pressure became too much for some and led them down the pathway of depression.

If you haven't seen it, I encourage you to watch the recent documentary film called *The Weight of Gold*. It is about depression and suicide among some of the most revered heroes on the planet—Olympic gold medalists. These athletes at the height of success are also prone to debilitating depression, even to the point of becoming suicidal. It is a powerful reminder how those who are outwardly successful can still be broken on the inside. In the luxury lifestyle space, I have met many successful, wealthy individuals who seemed to have it all but deep inside were severely depressed, which led some to even commit suicide.

I saw my own father struggle with depression for years and have seen how it can derail hopes and dreams for people and those around them. I encourage all of us to first and foremost be mindful about the people around us because we do not know what darkness they may be experiencing behind their outward appearance. Be the light in the darkness because at the end of the day, all that really matters in terms of your legacy is how you treated people and what positive impacts you made.

Your Spirit: Spiritual Health

When the COVID-19 global pandemic was at its worst, it seemed as if this new scourge might break the collective spirit of humanity. Thankfully, it did not. Think about how hopeless it seemed when the media was reporting death tolls rising faster than anyone had seen in their lifetime. It was downright scary. And yet even in those darkest hours, we witnessed much of humanity rise to meet a very difficult challenge. Think about the tireless dedication of medical and healthcare professional going above and beyond, even at great risk to themselves, to do whatever they could. Who will ever forget the images of people everywhere coming out of their homes to applaud and cheer and bang on pots and pans to express their gratitude for the doctors and nurses trying so desperately to keep people alive.

During those darkest of times, the human spirit showed its amazing resiliency. In part, I believe this came from a new realization of just how interconnected we all are, and how we must tap into our shared humanity to weather tough times together and soar to new heights.

How is your spirit these days? Are you making a positive impact on the world? Are you helping others? Are your dreams and vision aligned with your main values? If not, it's time to level up!

You've probably seen inspirational or motivational quotes on the internet. Notice how often they are accompanied by an image of a person standing on a mountain top, arms raised in victory. There's something about reaching the top of a mountain that's inherently good for the human spirit. It's a powerful metaphor often used to describe any especially meaningful occurrence, which might be called a "peak experience" or a "mountain-top moment." There's nothing quite like it. I encourage everyone to have such experiences to tap into their spiritual power to help fuel the journey toward their vision.

There are also lower-key spiritual moments that are just as important, such as guided breath meditation to be fully aware of the present moment. Practices like this help us remember to live our best lives right here, right now because this present moment is all we have. As we go through our own morning and daily routines, we must remind ourselves of our main values. We must treat everyone with dignity and respect. Our vision and our why take center stage and remind us what we're doing all this for. Then we set our intentions and act on our goals to make the most of each day. And we're always finding ways to express how truly grateful we are for everything and everyone in our lives.

Let me express my gratitude to *you* for reading this book. I hope it inspires and motivates you to start living your best life now. *Level Up* is all about relentless focus and commitment to improving ourselves every single day. Do that and your spirit will soar higher than you ever thought possible. Reaching new heights *is* within your power, and I hope you'll commit to dreaming big and making it happen. As Oprah Winfrey said, "The biggest adventure you can ever take, is to live the life of your dreams," and it is my wish for all of us!

CONCLUSION

Stories can have powerful impacts, especially on young children. One I will never forget is a story my father used to tell me—one that his father used to tell him. It goes like this:

Each evening before bedtime, a young boy would go outside and throw rocks at the moon.

His father asked him, "My son, why are you throwing rocks at the moon? You will never be able to reach it."

The boy smiled and said, "I know I will never reach the moon, but as I keep throwing these stones, my arm will get stronger and stronger."

This simple little story, passed down through generations of my family, illustrates the reason why we must always keep dreaming bigger regardless of what other people may say. It is only when we strive for dreams and goals beyond what seem possible today that we can truly level up to a more beautiful life tomorrow. If we aim for the moon in the here and now, we'll go much farther than we ever thought possible, especially if we also use tools and practices to drive forward momentum:

- **Vision:** Clearly defining a bold dream for the life we want to live.

- **Why:** Identifying the motivators that drive us onward and upward.
- **Wheel of Life:** Continuous self-improvement in all aspects of life.
- **Values:** Committing to virtuous ways of living.
- **Mindset:** Being positive and enthusiastic in all we do.
- **Goals:** Setting goals and achieving them to move us forward.
- **Habits:** Stacking effective habits to accelerate progress.
- **Routines:** Launching each day with an optimal morning routine.
- **Relationships:** Adding value by serving others.

Thank you for reading about this exciting journey so far—you are now a part of it! When I look back at the path my life has followed, I am greatly humbled by the support and encouragement I have received, even as I made mistake after mistake or encountered obstacles along the way. We can all turn obstacles into superpowers and level up to a wonderful life, but only if we surround ourselves with a network of positive, encouraging people. Let's all support each other so that #TogetherWeLevelUp to new heights!

APPENDIX:
HABITS TO LEVEL UP

Here is a robust list of habits for you to consider adopting. I've collected these from all over the place, including many books I've read or listened to, presentations and events I've attended, people I've talked to, and some I created myself. Some are ones I've already adopted myself while others are waiting in the wings for me to implement them. There are a lot of great ideas in here, so feel free to start picking and choosing ones you feel are going to help you reach new heights. And keep in mind the compound effect each habit you adopt will have over time. In fact, I highly recommend you read *The Compound Effect: Jumpstart Your Income, Your Life, Your Success* by Darren Hardy. It will get you excited about adopting habits to accelerate your journey onward and upward to new heights.

- The DNA of your success is in your routines. Make marginal adjustments to your daily routine to develop new habits and accomplish new goals
- Each morning, think of at least three things for which you are grateful.
- Apply the 30-second rule: After every meeting, lecture, experience, etc., take 30 seconds to write down the most important things about it.

- After meeting someone interesting, immediately follow up with a text, email, or video message containing an idea or something of value to the person.
- Give at least one compliment every day.
- *Smile!* You are stronger when you smile.
- Write down your dreams. It helps to study them and understand what your subconscious mind is trying to tell you.
- Apply the Pomodoro technique throughout your day.
- Answer the following question every morning when you wake up: Who needs me?
- Be like a tree: absorb negativity, exhale positivity.
- Make people feel significant.
- Say "thank you" to those who like, comment on, or share your content.
- Watch the words you use as they can determine your emotions and therefore your destiny.
- Before you go to bed, write down three things that happened during the day for which you are grateful.
- Change negative words for strong ones. For example, instead of "fear" say "excitement" or "nervited" (nervous and excited).
- The quality of your life will be dependent on the choices you make in the painful moments.
- Always give recognition to others.
- Be 100% accountable for everything in your life.
- Seek help daily, as no one succeeds alone.
- To influence people, talk about what they want and show them how to get it.
- You don't have to be great to get started, but you need to get started to be great: *Take action now.*
- Focus on daily self-improvement (you don't conquer the mountain, you conquer yourself).

- Build partnership and endorsement opportunities weekly.
- Bruce Johnson: "Your life is perfectly designed to produce the result you are currently getting." So, start making better adjustments on your daily habits.
- Focus on your posture as it will determine your physiology, which in turn will trigger your emotions and therefore your actions.
- Motion creates emotion, and 95% of our actions are based on emotions. So, *move!*
- Decide to be an appointment-setting, value-delivering, trust-building machine.
- Ask your partner every morning: "What can I help you with today?"
- Don't tolerate what you don't want in your life. Your life will be based on what you tolerate.
- Place an important note/reminder next to your alarm/phone (placed outside of your room) so when you wake up you automatically focus on something important, which puts you in power mode.
- Identify what/who you want to attract to your life and focus on who you must become to attract them.
- What is your territory in life? Invest in it, work on it, and make it your powerful place (like Arnold Schwarzenegger with the gym).
- Congratulate five people on their accomplishments and/or their great work daily.
- See through the eyes of love and bring positive energy to the world.
- Focus on actually winning and not just on looking like you are winning: *Be real* with yourself.
- Benjamin Franklin once said, "Those who trade freedom for security deserve neither," meaning if you trade happiness for money, you end up losing both.

- Treat everyone equally regardless of their status or relationship to you.
- Don't talk about someone unless they are in the room with you, meaning avoid gossip.
- Make the person you are talking to feel empowered (give compliments).
- Always invest in yourself first: CNEI (constant never ending improvement).
- Set your own rules and stay disciplined to them.
- Rest at the end, not in the middle.
- Pain always leaves a gift. Embrace it!
- What would you do if you knew you could not fail? Whatever that is, do it!
- Train hard: Those who sweat in training bleed less in war.
- Are you living life as a reaction to somebody else's actions? Start taking control of yourself.
- Positive energy is the current currency for personal and professional success.
- If it doesn't bring you money or value, hire someone to do it.
- One of the simplest and yet most powerful ways to get started on something is by repeating the words "Do it now! Do it now! Do it now!" over and over to yourself.
- Track every area you want to improve in your life and make adjustments as needed.
- Create and foster unity by approaching everyone with "us/we" instead of "you/I."
- "What I write I invite," so write down all your positive thoughts, ideas, and goals.
- Make everyone in a conversation feel important, not just the celebrities.
- Give something away to someone every day.

- Practice the art of journaling (your thoughts, what you did today, and how can you improve tomorrow).
- Never complain and never explain.
- When starting to work on a new habit, keep in mind the compound effect and have patience and consistency from the beginning.
- Invert everything you possibly can, meaning ask yourself what you *don't* want rather than what you *do* want.
- Use your bed only to sleep and make love.
- Compassion creates connection, so be compassionate to yourself and others.
- Focus on the "increase/improve" mentality with everything you do for yourself and others.
- Always deliver the unexpected (the "wow" factor).
- Practice daily the art of persistence: "I will persist, I will win."
- Make a "thank you list" of people you want to thank every day.
- Prepare your day the night before.
- Set the bar of your own expectations above what others expect of you.
- Build and nurture relationships every day, not only when you need them.
- Lead with questions, not answers.
- Always ask questions to experts.
- Eat healthy foods and ask yourself why you eat what you eat.
- When you agree to do something, do not complain about anything. Instead, move forward with a smile, energy, and positivity.
- Just like in a judo match, don't get upset at your competition in real life when you get hurt. It's just part of the game.

- Look at your goals in reverse engineering mode by focusing on the end results and then work it backwards to determine the path to get there.
- Turn stress into challenges to grow and increase health.
- Failure will never overtake me if my determination to succeed is strong enough.
- Apply "breadcrumbing," which means to share little pieces on what's happening in your world daily.
- Think in terms of possibilities and not failures, as if you can only succeed.
- Always take what others expect from you and then deliver better than what's expected.
- "Action may not always bring happiness, but there is no happiness without action." ~ Benjamin Disraeli
- Tomorrow is a bonus, not a fact. Therefore, enjoy each day and be grateful.
- Start conversations by asking questions to learn what someone wants and identify ways to bring them value.
- Always show up for those who are suffering or in need.
- Plan your finish time for the day and stick to it.
- Reach for failure. That's where growth exists.
- Be the last one to speak. Hold your thoughts/opinions until everyone else has spoken. Listen first and ask questions.
- Fail early, fail often, fail forward.
- Let your actions speak louder than your words.
- Spend one extra hour a day studying your field and in less than five years you will be an expert.
- Self-discipline starts with self-love. Love yourself and only focus on doing the things that are good for you.
- Ask yourself not what you want in life, but that for which are you willing to suffer.
- Pay attention to your physiology (how you stand, etc.) to create confidence and positive emotions.

- When you are suffering, embrace it, understand it, and go through it to make you stronger (never avoid it).
- Focus on the processes and not just on the result.
- When you help someone, always invest your time and energy in addition to money. Always invest all three, not just one or two of them.
- Listen when someone is talking to you.
- Surround yourself with the people and things you want in life.
- Use your ego as a tool, not a prison.
- Integrity is a key skill of a leader. Always be honest and tell the truth to yourself and to others.
- You may be wrong even when you think you are right, and that's okay.
- Care only about what matters, and don't waste time or energy on the rest.
- When you fail at something or it goes wrong, react with a positive attitude, as this is the world telling you something better is coming.
- Learn how to ask the good questions.
- Avoid insecurities.
- Apply "burst breathing" when angry or stressed.
- Apply "Context Concept" by studying/working/practicing in different places once in a while rather than always in the same place.
- "Read your own book." Don't run away from the truth. Be brutally honest with yourself and ask yourself how you can improve.
- Learn quickly what makes a group or person tick and try to provide it as soon as possible.
- Manage your systems, not the people.
- "Your reality is your creation." You are the master of your reality, so don't let any circumstance affect you. Instead, laugh about it and find a positive angle on it.

- Don't take anything personally.
- Always address someone by their name.
- Focus on your to "stop list" for the items/projects/ costs you need to stop.
- Have empathy and look at things from the other person's point of view.
- Create the right environments to release the right chemicals.
- Sleep well for 6–7 hours every night.
- Drink a gallon of water per day.
- Maintain good posture while walking and sitting.
- Instead of texting or emailing, send people audio messages or video selfies.
- Keep your Powerbase informed on what's happening in the market that matters to them (within your industry).
- Delegate as much responsibility as possible.
- Give, give, give, and then ask.
- Always keep it short, fast, and direct (you will always win + it is more polite).
- Revise your own agenda and visualize/prepare for any problem that may arise.
- Create your own persona that can't easily be categorized. Be interesting, charismatic, but still mysterious.
- Avoid analysis paralysis and take action (with calculated risks).
- Finish your high-priority items before noon.
- Set up the right expectations from the very beginning when you talk to someone.

Made in the USA
Columbia, SC
23 June 2023

18442741R00102